MW00901686

A STUDY OF EFFECTIVE CHEEK-TURNING, NEIGHBOR-LOVING AND SWORD-TO-PLOWSHARE CONVERSION

THE PEACE CLASS

by DIANA HADLEY and DAVID WEATHERSPOON

Della,

David & I value your friendship so much. We hope you will enjoy our reflections about teaching nonviolence.

Diana

978-1505721645 The Peace Class

Interior and Cover Design: Lindsay Hadley

Cover Image: Tim Lisko

THE PEACE CLASS *A study of effective cheek-turning, neighbor-loving and sword-to-plowshare conversion*

DEDICATED TO

Sarah and Norah Weatherspoon.

Clark and Lindsay Hadley.

The people who courageously put their lives on the line for the cause of peace.

ACKNOWLEDGEMENTS

From the beginning we have appreciated the encouragement from family and friends who thought we had a story and a cause to share.

William Bridges volunteered to edit our thoughts and did so with the gentle hand of professional and friend who organized and improved our words without changing the message or tone of the authors.

Thanks to Lindsay Hadley and Tim Lisko for the cover design, to Lindsay Hadley for the book design, and to Evan Finch for analyzing and suggesting title choices that would best describe our project.

Daniel Gates and Edward Chkwana agreed to share experiences, and Ann Barton, Clark Hadley and Sarah Weatherspoon read the manuscript for a final check before publication.

We are also grateful to guest speakers who shared their experiences and insights and students who learned with us as we explored nonviolent history and strategies.

Table of Contents

WHAT IT REALLY TAKES . . . .
FORWARD BY BILL BRIDGES

Anyone who expects this book to be a formula for a quick packaged class on non-violence is likely to be disappointed. It's something better— a report from the front by two busy people with many commitments, written in bits and pieces, over many months. I think of it as a Quaker quilt, put together from bright scraps during rare moments of reflection. I was lucky to be enlisted early as "an editor" for the project (there were others). "Editor" is in quotes because this was different from any other job in a long career of writing and editing. An editor's job is often to rein in or redirect the writer, improve organization and grammar, and make the work flow more evenly. A good editor tries to retain the writer's "voice," but the finished piece is expected to be smooth and seamless.

Some of this editing happened, but *The Peace Class* isn't that kind of book. An early suggested subtitle, which may or may not have survived, was *At War With Reality*. That suggested to me something written from the middle of a struggle, by the light of flashes in the night. Is it appropriate to use a war metaphor for teaching peace and nonviolence? I think so, if only because there are few metaphors for the tough, dirty work of confronting the "reality" of violence and aggression.

And how can we not think of that as the reality? We're surrounded by it, from the morning paper to the late-night television wrap-up. We see it in the endless cycle of video games, cop shows, and violent movies. We see it in the house down the street. Is this us?

The premise of this book is that this isn't, and doesn't have to be, the only reality. And that peace is hard, active work—not a classroom exercise. It takes determination and courage, even or especially from those of us who don't feel especially courageous.

Many years ago, the *Christian Science Monitor* posed a question, in a series of articles: "What if peace broke out?" The world did not immediately leap to embrace the Monitor's program, but some people have remembered it, as well as the countless other proposals for how we might live more humanely in the world. Someone has to imagine it first.

That's what David and Diana are doing in this book—imagining out of their own lives and teaching experience how a more humane world might evolve, person by person. Numbers and class sizes have nothing to do with it. Persistence and a certain cheerful subversiveness have everything to do with it. The writers mention how their class, even while attracting students in good numbers, eventually fell victim to the exigencies of campus financing. At that point, they could have thrown up their hands or spent their energies in castigating the budgeters, who were, after all, good people just trying to make ends meet.

Instead, they did something novel. They taught the class on their own time, one evening a week, for no pay or credit, to whoever showed up. Class members and others brought food as an incentive. The numbers were never big, but the idea survived. At another time, maybe in another place, the "peace class" will rise again.

You, reader, may be one of those leading it. If you do, you will not be following this book as a syllabus or perhaps even as a guide. You will be looking into your own heart and experience, in the place you happen to find yourself, and imagining, "What if . . . ."

A few months ago, I found myself listening to a woman named Jackie from Nashville, Tenn., who is part of a church group that spends time with second graders in the city's worst slums—very violent places. She mentioned that the state (and other states, too) have found failure in the second grade to be a reliable indicator of future prison needs. "Prisoners can't read," she said. Her group has been able to help the kids a little, "but we need more people. We have lots of folks who will send money, but who won't drive across town to help us in the schools." She paused and reflected. Then she added, "What it really takes is love."

01
WHEN THE TEACHER IS THE STUDENT
BY DIANA HADLEY

"Unless we teach our children peace,
somebody else will teach them violence."

—*Coleman McCarthy, I Would Rather Teach Peace*

Sometimes the teacher learns as much or more than the students, and that's part of the story about teaching nonviolence. Before designing a curriculum for a college peace class, I'd already completed a rewarding 33-year career that included teaching high-school English, speech, and journalism and advising a student newspaper, yearbook, and broadcast team. I was excited to move to a job at a small liberal-arts college where I could remain connected to an academic environment without evenings and weekends of grading papers and attending extracurricular events. This was to be the part of my life when I could pursue other interests, and volunteering for peace initiatives was at the top of my to-do list.

After a couple of months of this new freedom, I realized I had two problems. I had not found my "peace niche," and I missed interaction with students. My friend Sylvia gave me Coleman McCarthy's book *I Would Rather Teach Peace,* and about the same time I discovered there was an opportunity to create a liberal-arts course for a four-week winter-term session. I began the search for other peace syllabi and resources. It seemed like the perfect solution.

I thought it would be easier.

I always enjoyed the creativity and energy involved in designing curricula, but this was a challenge. During a search on a bookstore computer, I found a book title I thought was promising. Next to a brief description of the book was the information: "Location in store: peace shelf."

I knew the layout of my favorite bookstore, and I had never seen a peace shelf. After a thorough search, I snagged an employee and asked if he could help me find the peace shelf. He looked at me as if I'd just landed from a far-away planet and said, "Ma'am, we don't have a peace shelf." When he read the disappointment on my face, he added with enthusiasm, "But we have a whole section on war!" The words, "And I think that's the problem with this world," had already left my mouth before I returned to a more peaceful tone and said I appreciated his help anyway.

One of the first personal lessons in my teaching-peace journey was the realization that the number of books, movies, television shows, and other resources about war don't just outnumber peace choices; they outnumber them exponentially. Even though I usually designed curriculum for semester courses, I wondered how I would find enough material for four weeks.

I looked up Coleman McCarthy's contact information and called a number, hoping to find a peace staff that could direct me. When Mrs. McCarthy answered the phone and spent time sharing some of their favorite resources, I realized I was trying to become part of a small group. But I also felt her enthusiasm about the endeavor and encouragement to do something so important.

And that was when I began to evaluate my ability to teach such a class.

In addition to my teaching experience, I had rationalized that my Quaker background was an asset. However, more reflection made me realize that the Quaker peace testimony was a small part of my life experience compared to the culture of the small rural community where I grew up. My dad, his brothers, and many of the men I knew were World War II veterans. My childhood narrative was that they fought the war "to bring down Hitler and the evil Germans and Japanese." Some of them had tattoos of U.S. flags and fierce-looking eagles. My elementary-school teachers promoted unquestioned patriotism. Our history books emphasized wars, and the Cold War of the 1950s sustained a fear of other countries and the probability of fighting another war. We practiced getting under our desks in case of nuclear attack, and the family of a friend built an underground shelter just in case.

It didn't take much research, several decades later, to discover that the inclusion of nonviolence as a study in schools wasn't much greater than my own experience. Surely a class that provided ways to think about conflict resolution would be a positive addition to anyone's education. I concluded that I wasn't an expert, but I believed in the moral ground of peaceful approaches to conflict. Nonviolent actions might not always work, but it was important to witness to them anyway.

The teacher had much to learn.

I was excited when the college approved the course, but my anxiety increased as winter term approached. I wasn't teaching at one of Indiana's traditional peace colleges where a class about nonviolence is preaching to the choir. My students might not embrace the concepts, and there was a possibility they would be offended by the suggestion that violence could be eliminated with anything but more violence. I was reminded that when the high school where I taught tried to discourage fighting by saying that everyone involved was at fault, many parents pushed back and said, "I tell my kid that if someone hits him, he can hit back no matter what the rule is."

I remembered that soldiers were heroes, and pacifists were wimps or cowards in the community where I grew up and the town where I taught for 33 years—and that it was similar to the communities of students who had signed up for my class. When I told one of my colleagues about the class, he said, "That should be interesting," and added that while he really liked Quakers, he really didn't get that "turn the other cheek thing."

Oh, oh.

On the first day of class, I gave a quick survey to see how much my 25 students knew about violent and nonviolent historical events. It turned out to be a good activity to begin discussion. Most had studied every war on the list at some point in their education. While a few had heard of Gandhi, specifics about him or even the American civil rights movement were sketchy. I decided that the glass-half-full take on this exercise was that the course was bound to include new information for them. It didn't seem likely that anyone was going to claim he had already covered any of the material extensively.

Launching any class involves an assessment of teaching strategies and materials as "keep" and "throw away" for the next time around. The day I presented a quick lesson about Sadako Sasaki, famous for her peace crane project, I also passed out directions and materials to make origami peace cranes as a hands-on activity before a break in the 2½-hour class.

I worried that young men in college would just refuse to do it. However, the good sports worked hard though not always successfully. One guy struggled for several minutes before wadding up the paper and tossing it aside. Then he laughed at himself for taking it so seriously. It gave me a chance to emphasize that peace activities take patience. I was surprised when he returned early from his break to try again and succeed. This simple in-class project didn't just provide a change of pace; it helped all of us appreciate Sasaki's effort and the influence her story generated. It was a "keep."

I tinkered with the syllabus as the days passed. Feedback was positive, and I was enjoying the challenge. It wasn't until the end of the 4-week term that I experienced the most personally profound moment of my teaching career. On the next-to-last day, after we had reviewed material for the last test, I asked if there were other questions. I responded to a couple of easy ones, and then a young man asked if I thought there were any situations when a nonviolent approach to conflict couldn't work?

I was stunned. After just four weeks studying nonviolent actions, one of my students was asking a question I had never asked myself. The very question reflected a buy-in beyond anything I had ever considered. For me, a nonviolent strategy was the best moral approach, but could it also be the most effective approach to end all conflicts?

I've never been afraid to tell my students I don't know the answer to a question. I just admit ignorance and make it a class challenge with a humble but enthusiastic: "I don't know. Let's find out." But no student had ever asked a question that affected me so powerfully. I told him I didn't have an answer, but that we should all think about the question and discuss it the next day. That question has remained as the class evolved to a semester and improved with the addition of David Weatherspoon as a team teacher. Searching for the answer is the story of the rest of this book.

02
FAITH, HOSPITALITY, AND NONVIOLENCE
BY DAVID WEATHERSPOON

"Blessed are the peacemakers for they will be called the children of God."

—Matthew 5:9

Diana has written that teachers often learn as much as their students; this is one reason I said yes when she asked me to join her in teaching a semester-long course in nonviolence. As the campus minister, I knew something about nonviolence, but I wanted to learn more. It was clear from some of our conversations that we would work well together in the classroom. Our styles, combined with our passion for nonviolence and justice, meshed well.

My faith background compels me to take the life of Jesus very seriously, and also take seriously the religious giants of other faiths. At the heart of almost every major faith tradition is a hospitality code that demands welcoming and caring for the stranger. This theme of hospitality is displayed time and again in the Biblical text, through parables like that of the Good Samaritan, through the Beatitudes, and in the often-quoted Matthew 25 text when Jesus speaks of welcoming the stranger, feeding the hungry, and giving drink to the thirsty. He notes that those who do these things are truly welcoming Jesus himself. To withhold hospitality from another is, in fact, to do violence to the Christ.

As I discovered in seminary, Jesus' teachings in the Sermon on the Mount (Matthew 5:38-48) illustrate how to resist an assailant and how to actively struggle against injustice and against enemies without using violence. These teachings became the basis for Gandhi in his struggle for civil rights in South Africa and India, and later for Martin Luther King Jr. in his own struggle for those rights in the United States. Being struck on one cheek and simply turning the other has appeared to many as a meek and even a weak response. However, as theologian Walter Wink has noted, this act is any-thing but weak. In ancient times, a slave would be struck only with the back of the hand. To strike someone with the open hand was to treat the person as an equal. Therefore, turning the other cheek was an active resistance that said, "I demand to be treated equally. When you hit me again, use your open hand." It also demonstrated that the spirit of the offended could not simply be stamped out by humiliation tactics.

The same is true with carrying the load of a Roman soldier a second mile. There were literal markers for how far a Roman soldier could demand that someone carry his belongings. However, the person who defied this rule and carried the load a second mile once again showed the strength of his belief that such Roman tactics would not work—the insult was actually reversed. Nothing is clearer than offering the cloak as well as the coat. Poor people who had literally nothing else to spare could have their coat taken for the day as a means of taxation or of shaming them and keeping them in their societal place. At the end of the day, their coat was returned only to be taken away the following day to continue the patronizing cycle. Jesus suggests a change to the cycle by offering the cloak as well because the cloak would be the only garment left to hide their nakedness once the coat had been taken. The effect of removing the cloak would be to flip the shame upon the oppressor and alter such unjust actions. Loving enemies further disorients them. Oppressors know how to use force and have the power to do so when met with hate and violence, but they're caught off guard by those who return acts of violence and humiliation with nonviolent strength and love.

What I have just shared is the theological framework that troubled me. I say troubled because I find numbers of people who claim to be Christians but few who practice the teachings. Perhaps they lack knowledge of Jesus' instructions on how to nonviolently remain strong and steadfast in the face of oppression. However, the teachings and the calls to hospitality are quite clear about loving one's neighbor and the enemy. Equally clear are the Beatitudes, particularly "Blessed are the peacemakers, for they shall be called children of God." These teachings are challenging, and I have struggled and continue to struggle to try to love in response to hate. It's difficult to step out of a cycle of violence and offer a new way, and too many times I've failed to live up to the challenges my faith demands of me as a follower.

Co-teaching the class with Diana, I have discovered a wealth of Christians and people of other faith traditions who take their faith quite seriously and model what it means to live it out even in the face of some of the most violently oppressive regimes and tactics. It has renewed my own faith and hope as well as kindled a desire to teach these ancient nonviolent principles to students, who at first view them as bizarre and unrealistic. Then in the class they realize many of their peers elsewhere are practicing nonviolent strategies and having great success transforming cultures of violence. These peaceful strategies don't get the media spotlight that acts of violence do in living rooms around the globe.

The world is full of fear and anxiety. Much of the fear has been purposely generated to sustain economies built on violence. But the answer cannot be to begin more wars and continue to build larger armies. The buildup of weaponry, drone attacks, and clandestine operations will only serve to alienate and create mistrust and greater violence. It is an unsustainable end.

Engagement and dialogue are cornerstones of nonviolence, and they are rays of hope and light in a global community very much in need of alternatives to current courses of action. The way of hospitality that is the hallmark of all the great faith traditions is the only viable option. Hospitality provides a way to make room at the table for everyone in the global community, and this space is created by nonviolent means.

03
WHAT I LEARNED AS A CHILD

BY DAVID WEATHERSPOON

"We must begin to inoculate our children against militarism by educating them ... I would rather teach peace than war, love rather than hate."

—Albert Einstein, Theoretical Physicist

Where does one begin looking for an alternative when the airwaves are permeated with reports of violence and injustice? For me, it begins with a look at my faith journey. The life of Jesus has served as my model of the exemplary path to freedom and justice, and the path of his life was one of stringent nonviolence. I am not alone in this revelation. Both Gandhi and King formed their principles of nonviolence upon the foundation provided by the stories of Jesus in the Gospels. However, it did not immediately click for me that my faith and my culture were at odds.

Growing up, I learned quickly to believe that we live in a Christian country, and the drumbeat of "God is on our side" began at an early age. While hearing tales of church and state, I came to find that the two were intricately linked. Venture into nearly any church, and one would find an American flag prominently displayed. Listen to any military oath and one would hear a call to protect "God and country." The Pledge of Allegiance said, "One nation, under God, indivisible . . . ." God and nation were inseparable, and even a small child could quickly grasp that God liked us best. Violence that occurred in the world was the result of random acts by deranged individuals or by misguided nations. The United States would use violence only as a last resort; if it did, it was certainly justified as God's chosen light unto the world.

But violence was always being portrayed on the nightly news, which I watched faithfully with my grandparents. The rhetoric of Vietnam, American hostages in Iran, Sandinistas, "guerrillas," Star Wars missile strategy, Cold War, Soviets, and Iran-Contra were constants. I did not know these people who were causing such an uproar, but it was clear we had to be ready to fight them at a moment's notice. The "guerrillas" sounded particularly menacing to a young boy growing up in rural America. Some of my earliest memories were pictures of American hostages being held in Iran; tension and fear filled the room over the dire circumstances of the hostages— and of all of us, for that matter, with the potential of another war looming.

Other strange and violent events were happening. The news broke that John Lennon had been shot. I was five, but I remember the people around me being moved and outraged by his death. Others commented that "he was just another hippie," deeming his message and personhood as of less worth than others. Just a couple years later, President Reagan was shot but survived. It was a very violent national scene.

On the personal level, I was never encouraged to start a fight, but I could retaliate if someone hit me first. There were many fights, particularly of the family variety, with nephews who were closer in age to me than my own siblings. Many of these began because we were imitating the wrestlers we loved to watch: Jake the Snake, Hulk Hogan, Randy Macho Man Savage, Andre the Giant, and others. Someone would get hurt, and the real brawl would start. Spankings by my father would ensue. Even the play could be violent.

So what did we make of the teachings of Jesus? After all, we all agreed that we were on his team. But some of his teachings sounded a little weak. Why not give those Romans what was coming to them? How dare someone harm the only innocent one in the room? So the sermons would appeal to the sense that the persecutors would get what was coming to them. It would be when angry and scary Jesus returned and cast everyone in the lake of fire who wasn't on his team, and you better believe that time would be soon.

The focus in the church I attended had very little to do with the life of Jesus. The brunt of attention was the death of Jesus, and that he had died for all the sins of the world. The only way to forgiveness was to accept this as fact so that we might receive resurrection as Jesus had. Otherwise, anyone who had not accepted this truth was sure to meet a violent and terrible demise. Sermons had to end with a trip to the cross, the need for redemption, and a promise of paradise to follow. The life of Jesus was only a preface to the real story, or so it seemed.

This is what I learned in church.

04
A SAFE PLACE
TO DISCOVER GRAY
BY DIANA HADLEY

"In a republican nation, whose citizens are to be led by reason and persuasion and not by force, the art of reasoning becomes of first importance."

—*Thomas Jefferson, U.S. President*

As a freshman at a large university, I once took a biology class with 500 students—and we were only one of three such sections. One class had the live professor, but I never saw him except as the flickering gray image on a small TV screen. There was no class discussion, and our grades depended on multiple-choice tests.

It all worked after a fashion, but how dull, for the students and probably the professor, too! I'm sure he would envy David and me, who teach in a situation that allows us flexibility with curriculum and teaching strategies. We don't have to teach to a test or look out at overbooked classes of students we'll never get to know. We're also never bored because each group of students brings a different chemistry and different challenges.

That's not to say that we hit a home run with every class. Sometimes our students don't finish reading assignments or respond enthusiastically to the approach we've selected. They may not have the life experience to understand or appreciate the material, and we may not know them well enough to adjust the message for them. But it's important in a class about nonviolence that we creatively explore ways to communicate with 25 people as a group and individually.

We try to provide a "safe place" for students to talk about their questions, doubts, and the faith they grew up with at home—and to begin the inevitable transition from a black-and-white world to one with endless shades of gray.

I didn't experience much gray until my first year in college in 1967. My parents were Quakers, and I lived that faith without question for the beginning of my life. I was moved by the stories of Quakers who tried to reduce suffering during World Wars I and II, efforts that led to a Nobel Peace Prize for the British and American Friends Service Committees.

As a college student I evaluated my own faith and others, not because I was looking for something else, but because I was curious. Many of my new friends didn't support the Vietnam War; some didn't support any war. My home Quaker connections included more veterans than conscientious objectors. The first time I shared reservations about the war, I realized my new opinions weren't appreciated in my old community. I was looking at events with fresh eyes, but "my country right or wrong" was still the rule at home. I wrestled with this dilemma, but only voiced my opinion in safe places. I was trying to be the good kid who didn't pick up bad ideas from the big world. It wasn't an honest or courageous decision, but it kept me in good standing.

Because of this background, I try to make my classroom a safe place for students to discover and discuss the gray areas as they search for the truths of their lives. It's especially important to create such a place in a class about nonviolence. Many have never questioned their beliefs about violence. As they learn the historical and cultural significance of "turning the other cheek" and "an eye for an eye," they need a place where they can share their questions—any questions—and challenge new information without fear of criticism.

Students may say some outrageous things as they meet new concepts, but open and civil discussion generally leads to rational conclusions. David and I often tell our students that we're not trying to tell them what to think; we just want them to think.

Of course, there are some right and wrong answers in any class, including one about nonviolence. But the goal is to introduce students to significant historical events and the people who brought them about—and then evaluate the gray areas together.

I eventually made a conscious decision to embrace Quakerism even though I could have been comfortable in other faiths that also promoted peace. I also found an admiration for people of other faiths who speak for peace in times of war. What an irony that they find themselves in conflict when they speak against violence!

Desmond Doss was one of these people. He wasn't a member of one of the traditional "peace churches," but this Seventh-Day Adventist believed "Thou shall not kill" was a commandment he could not break even for a war that most people thought was necessary. Those who served with him in World War II berated as cowardly this medic who would not carry a gun—until he single-handedly rescued more than 75 wounded men who had been under heavy fire for many hours.

Doss was the first conscientious objector to receive the Medal of Honor. Terry Benedict's documentary about this quiet unassuming hero includes touching interviews with Doss's comrades who regretted the way they had treated him once they realized he was the bravest man in their unit. A friend of mine who served in the military during the Vietnam War made similar comments about the conscientious objectors he knew who served as medics.

Peace activists have used a variety of ways to challenge war, from Doss's quiet service to the dramatic sacrifice of Norman Morrison, a 31-year-old Baltimore Quaker who set himself on fire at the Pentagon in 1965 to protest the Vietnam War. Decades later, Robert McNamara, secretary of defense for Presidents John Kennedy and Lyndon Johnson, spoke with sadness and admiration about the conviction that made Morrison give his life in such a drastic and public way.

David and I don't encourage students to immolate themselves. I don't use the class to recruit Quakers, and as far as I know this approach has been a success. (Churches that produce high-interest multimedia messages accompanied by praise bands to inspire their members are tough competition for Quaker services that include long periods of silence.)

We do want our students to analyze many religions and individuals who have demonstrated peace, and to answer important questions:

- What were their motives and strategies?
- How can their actions be measured for success or failure?
- Does knowledge of the history of nonviolence help people navigate the present and the future?

If in the process of studying nonviolent actions and the people who participate in them, students find inspiration and tools to weave nonviolent initiatives into their own lives and faith traditions, a more peaceful world becomes possible.

Our class constantly humbles us. We won't forget a student who approached us early in one class and said, "Is this class going to be all about Jesus? Because if it is, I'm dropping it now." I deftly passed her to David, who explained the influence Jesus had in nonviolent movements, even among leaders such as Gandhi, who weren't Christian. We encouraged her to hang in and look for the links in the classes ahead.

We felt she would come around, but facial expression and body language stayed pretty much the same. Then at some point she began to change, and we didn't even see it happening. Toward the end of the semester we asked students if there were any practical ways they might incorporate things they had learned in class. We were surprised when the student who had complained earlier in the semester quickly volunteered, "This class has changed my life."

David and I held our collective breath. What was she going to say next? She explained that she had a job that required listening to the rants of angry customers. Because of the class, she said, she had begun reacting calmly and defusing the situation. She added that she felt better about herself and enjoyed the surprise of the customers when she didn't yell back at them.

David and I were just as surprised as her customers. We didn't know exactly when or how it occurred, but at some point, with or without Jesus, she had embraced some nonviolent strategies that improved her life and the lives of others. It was a moment that would never have happened in my freshman biology class. Here are some thoughts about the case for classes in nonviolence:

WHO SHOULD TAKE A NONVIOLENCE CLASS?

Answer: most people. The example above isn't unusual.

- Observe the approaches people use with others in business and social exchanges.
- Note the prevalence of local violence, abuse and road rage.
- Read letters to the editor and replies at the end of newspaper stories and blogs.
- Make a log of movies and television programming dividing the list into violent vs. nonviolent themes.
- Note the number of broken relationships among people you know: divorce and other family breakups, as well as organization, church, and workplace conflicts.
- Note the conflict in athletic events including Little League games.

Students begin to believe that more nonviolent, civil approaches to issues, from family squabbles to international crises, are not just the best moral choices but the most pragmatic ones as well, once they have had the opportunity to study them. Similarly, heroes without guns, from Gandhi to the young people who participated in Arab Spring, may take the place of Rambos once they are given equal time.

CAN EVERYONE TAKE A NONVIOLENCE CLASS?

Unfortunately, most middle school and high school students have had no training in conflict resolution, and the curriculum seldom includes much information about nonviolent movements even in history classes.

Some colleges offer nonviolence classes, even majors in nonviolence; but as colleges are urged to drop total credit hours for graduation, students will take fewer elective classes, the place where classes about nonviolence are often included.

WHAT DIFFERENCE DOES IT MAKE?

It's hard to know, but consider the following questions:

- How would the United States be different if elected officials took classes in nonviolence or conflict resolution in the two months between their election and the beginning of their term of office?
- How would decisions about international conflicts change if the country had a Secretary of Defense AND a Secretary of Peace?

A SECRETARY OF PEACE

BY DAVID WEATHERSPOON

Looking at an invitation list can give a real sense of who and what are valued at a party—or any other gathering.

When looking at the list of those invited to meetings of the President's Cabinet, one will find the vice president and the 15 departments and positions deemed necessary for the direction of the nation. The 15 include: Agriculture, Commerce, Defense, Education, Energy, Health and Human Services, Homeland Security, Housing and Urban Development, Interior, Labor, State, Transportation, Treasury, Veterans Affairs, and the Attorney General. Noticeable attention is given to domestic and foreign affairs as well as military strength. Absent from the list is a Secretary of Peace.

Proposing the addition of a Secretary of Peace to the Cabinet is not a new idea. Since the 1700s, when George Washington suggested legislation proposing a Department of Peace, the concept of adding a representative who could counter-balance the then-Department of War was considered important. Support at the time came from Thomas Jefferson, Benjamin Banneker, and Benjamin Rush. However, such legislation has never been adopted.

Clearly, providing a position for peace among the nation's chief advisers has been seen as very important. Groups such as Amnesty International and the United States Peace Institute still work with representatives such as Ohio Congressman Dennis Kucinich to re-emphasize the importance of a Department of Peace in this country. Kucinich has reintroduced legislation every two years since July 2001 to establish a Department of Peace and currently has 52 cosponsors.

To turn down the appeal of the first president and many intelligent and concerned citizens in the years since doesn't answer the question why? Is the presence of a peace secretary in the Cabinet, or a department that focuses on peace, really a threat to national interests? The nation's early historical focus upon manifest destiny and the ongoing desire to maintain the world's undisputedly dominant military force might mean that the answer to these questions is, "Yes, the presence of a Secretary of Peace is a definite threat." At least, it is seen as a threat to the unquestioned military-industrial complex. Whenever unrest occurs in the world, particularly in areas with an abundance of oil, military engagement is often seen as a first resort. To question the need for a military buildup can lead to accusations that the questioner is unpatriotic.

However, even President Washington knew that another voice was necessary in the conversation in order to maintain a healthy perspective on when to use the military and when to look for a true win-win situation for both parties through the pursuit of peace. A Secretary of Peace would continually seek the opportunity to preserve human dignity for all involved, and this would serve domestic and foreign interests much better than seeking ways to engage in warfare. It would be the counter-weight so often absent among the nation's top advisors. It is not a new concept. It is instead a necessary ideal as posited by our first president, an ideal that is long overdue for implementation. We need a Secretary of Peace.

05
WHAT WE KNOW THAT ISN'T SO
BY DAVID WEATHERSPOON

"Peace is not made at the council table
or by treaties, but in the hearts of men."

—Herbert Hoover, U.S. President

It's often called "critical thinking." Maybe so
often that the words have dulled our ears. "Careful
thinking" might be a better term, or perhaps just
"thinking." For our purposes, we ask students to
reflect on things they've always assumed were so,
but that turn out after careful study not to be.

Still, "critical thinking" is a familiar term, and useful. We use it here and
in the class. Our editor and friend who read our early remarks about the
atomic bomb said he questioned them immediately and felt like putting the
manuscript aside.

He had known all his life that the bombing of Hiroshima and Nagasaki was necessary to shorten the war and save American lives. But a few minutes of Googling disclosed some authoritative voices that said, in the words of the old song, "It ain't necessarily so." Some of those voices are quoted in Diana's essay that follows this one.

On the first day of our class in nonviolence, Diana and I go over the syllabus and clarify one point immediately. Our goal, we tell the students, is not to make you think like us, but to make each of you a critical thinker. Our hypothesis is that in becoming critical thinkers, you will become more nonviolent.

A few years ago, the world witnessed a horrific lack of critical thinking. A White House media campaign hammered at Iraq's possession of "weapons of mass destruction." If Saddam Hussein didn't hand over these weapons, the United States and its supporters would have to resort to military force.

Former President Jimmy Carter authored a column against the preemptive military action. There were significant protests worldwide, but only Barbara Lee, California congresswoman, voted against the resolution that would authorize the president almost unlimited military power.

Support for the invasion of Iraq dwindled as investigators failed to find WMDs. An outcry began around the world and in the United States protesting unnecessary aggression against Iraq. There was clearly no evidence that Saddam had anything to do with 9/11 or had any WMDs of the sort he supposedly was about to use. Even so, the United States began a war that it wrongly assumed would be short and incur few casualties.

In class, students are asked to examine all viewpoints in a conflict. We use resources from the Peace Learning Center in Indianapolis to help them learn to ask questions of potential aggressors, with the aim of dissuading them from violence. With listening and patience, most conflicts can be diplomatically resolved. As students realize the needs of all parties involved, and apply critical thinking, solutions begin to appear that allow all sides to win. Violence always demands that one side dominate the other, but in most cases neither side emerges as a winner in the long run. Damage to the dignity and humanity of participants in a violent conflict results in a net loss for all involved.

Students look at clips of nonviolent resistance, from the Nashville civil rights movement to Denmark's resistance to its Nazi occupiers. They're asked to consider the preparation, creativity, and thoughtfulness needed to engage a violent oppressor nonviolently. They soon realize that the Nashville protestors and the Danes would have been crushed if they had resorted to violence, and that they also would have surrendered the moral high ground to which their causes appealed. It takes much more thought and creativity to resist another with values and ideals than it does to ask them to submit to physical force. Only through the force of conscience can both sides be redeemed and preserve their personhood.

Once violence takes over both sides, critical thinking is rarely employed in a way that seeks to redeem both parties. Each side begins using language that demonizes the other. Each tries to justify its cause. The media become tools to persuade the masses that armed conflict is necessary. Most egregiously, anyone questioning those leading the charge may be seen as a traitor.

All these are major red flags in critical thinking. We teach our students to be aware of language that demonizes. Words like "terrorist," "infidel," "tyranny" and many others have been used through the centuries to dehumanize opponents. Whenever such terms are used, we should begin to ask good questions.

To think critically, one must look honestly at all the facts, whether the fault lies in the opponent or in the mirror. Truth can't be manufactured through media campaigns. Global outcries for restraint must not be ignored. Nonviolence teaches us to think counter-culturally to violent agendas. Thus critical thinking paves the way for nonviolent solutions to real problems by using facts and listening to global wisdom.

06
CASE STUDY: THE DROPPING OF THE A-BOMB
BY DIANA HADLEY

"Freedom is hammered out on the anvil of discussion, dissent and debate."

—Hubert H. Humphrey, U.S. Vice-President

IT'S TIME FOR A TEST. *Place a check beside each name or group of people who agreed that dropping atomic bombs on Japan was the right course of action to end WWII:*

○ Gen. Dwight Eisenhower

○ Albert Einstein

○ 69 scientists who worked on the Manhattan Project

○ Gen. Douglas MacArthur

○ Former President Herbert Hoover

ANSWER: *There should be no checks. None of the people or groups listed favored use of the atomic bomb at the end of World War II.*

Many Americans across generational lines are surprised by this information. Whether they remember the bombing of Hiroshima and Nagasaki or have studied it, do people have some sense that there was moral concern about killing women and children? The rationalization that has prevailed for more than six decades is that the bomb was necessary to end the war and save American lives.

There was no national discussion before the bombings because it was a secret project. A few historians have described the protests from some who had prior knowledge, including the 69 scientists who worked on the Manhattan Project and signed a petition against the bomb's use. But most U.S. history books follow the more patriotic line that it was necessary, and most students are led to believe that the United States sometimes has to make tough choices to do the right thing. Even the suggestion that the United States hasn't always done the right thing may not be appreciated or accepted.

Deborah Meier, an educator who speaks throughout the country, questions the direction of the U.S. education system. Meier, who has founded and directed schools in urban centers, says the current trend of instruction discourages students from developing skepticism and empathy. She adds that without those two traits democracy is in trouble. A more rigorous study of the decision to drop the atomic bomb is a way to incorporate both skepticism and empathy into the nonviolence curriculum.

Hiroshima's estimated death toll in the bombing and the first four months afterward was between 90,000 and 166,000. Nagasaki's toll was between 60,000 and 80,000. Roughly half those deaths occurred on the first day. Most were civilians.

It's important to look at the numbers to try to imagine the magnitude of the human destruction. It's also revealing to see quotes from people who were associated with or aware of the project and had differing views.

Stephen Walker's book Shockwave, published in 2005, provides an overview of the many people who were involved at different levels. Walker says that very few crew members who flew either of the two missions ever expressed guilt for what they had done, and he includes quotes that help us understand how they have managed to do that. Twenty years after the mission, pilot Paul Tibbets said, "I have absolutely no feeling of guilt. I was directed to do it."

U.S. military commanders didn't have the power to directly question orders and if the government ordered atomic bombs to be dropped, the U.S. military could not disobey. "The dropping of the atomic bomb was done by a military man under military orders. We're supposed to carry out orders and not question them," Gen. Carl Spaatz, commander of the U.S. Army Air Forces, said.

President Harry Truman stuck to his decision to drop the bombs until his death. When he heard about the bombing's success, he reportedly said, "This is the greatest thing in history." In reply to a religious group's opposition to further use of the bomb, he said, "Nobody is more disturbed over the use of the atomic bomb than I am, but I was greatly disturbed over the unwarranted attack by the Japanese on Pearl Harbor and their murder of our prisoners of war. The only language they seem to understand is the one we have been using to bombard them. When you have to deal with a beast you have to treat him as a beast."

According to Shockwave, one of the copilots of the Enola Gay, the plane that dropped the first bomb, described the mushroom cloud as "every color in the world . . . beautiful." But others who were part of that mission spoke very differently. Robert Shumard, one of the Enola Gay's assistant engineers, said, "There was nothing but death in that cloud. All those Japanese souls ascending to Heaven." Bob Lewis, another crew member, wrote in his log, "My God, what have we done? If I live for a hundred years, I will never quite get these few minutes out of my mind."

Walker's book is masterful in weaving the story of the bomb from the accounts of those who developed it, those who decided to drop it, those who did drop it, and those who survived. While the book is too long for class use in its entirety, choosing key events and quotes can still generate interest and valuable class discussion. From just a few quotes, students are engaged with questions:

- If a person's superior directs him to do something that seems wrong, is he innocent of the action?
- How hard is it to speak up when a majority action seems wrong?
- How can one effectively voice an unpopular opinion?
- Are people who avoid talking about their war service doing so because of what they saw—or what they did?
- Do the ends justify the means?
- Is there such a thing as a "just war?"

SOME GUIDELINES: In any discussion the teacher must provide direction and referee some moments as students begin to develop and share viewpoints. A few ground rules should be established at the beginning of the discussion regarding length of exchanges and respect for all speakers. Students should be challenged to identify their comments as facts or opinions. Helping them learn to analyze sources effectively will serve them for the rest of their lives.

As a journalism teacher it hurts me to say this, but many students have absorbed the media's confrontational approach to discussion. This seems to reward the loudest voice in the room, and it promotes a "but that's my opinion" attitude that has little regard for facts. The classroom provides a place to stop the action and check the facts.

Listed below are quotes that can generate positive discussion.

QUOTES FROM THOSE WHO KNEW ABOUT THE PROPOSED ATOMIC BOMBINGS OF JAPAN

"In 1945 Secretary of War [Henry] Stimson, visiting my headquarters in Germany, informed me that our government was preparing to drop an atomic bomb on Japan. I was one of those who felt that there were a number of cogent reasons to question the wisdom of such an act.... On the basis of my belief that Japan was already defeated and that dropping the bomb was completely unnecessary.... I thought [atomic bombs] were no longer mandatory as a measure to save American lives."

—*Dwight Eisenhower, Five-Star General and U.S. President*

"The Japanese had, in fact, already sued for peace. The atomic bomb played no decisive part, from a purely military point of view, in the defeat of Japan."

—*Fleet Admiral Chester W. Nimitz, Commander-in-chief of the U.S. Pacific Fleet*

"There was no military justification for the dropping of the bomb[s]. The war might have ended weeks earlier, if the United States had agreed, as it later did anyway, to the retention of the institution of the [Japanese] emperor."

—Douglas MacArthur, Five-Star General

"The use of [the atomic bombs] at Hiroshima and Nagasaki was of no material assistance in our war against Japan. The Japanese were already defeated and ready to surrender because of the effective sea blockade and the successful bombing with conventional weapons. . . . I was not taught to make war in that fashion, and wars cannot be won by destroying women and children."

—Fleet Admiral William D. Leahy, chief of staff to President Truman

"When we didn't need to do it, and we knew we didn't need to do it, and [Japan] knew that we knew we didn't need to do it, we used [Japan] as an experiment for two atomic bombs."

—Brigadier General Carter Clarke, U.S. Military Intelligence

"Prior to 31 December 1945 and in all probability prior to 1 November 1945, Japan would have surrendered even if the atomic bombs had not been dropped, even if the Soviet Union had not entered the war, and even if no invasion had been planned or contemplated."

—Paul Nitze, vice chairman, U.S. Strategic Bombing Survey

"If we were to go ahead with plans for an invasion, I believe the Japanese thought that they could inflict heavy casualties on us and as a result get better surrender terms. On the other hand if we told [Japan] that no invasion would take place, [Japan] would've surrendered."

—General Carl Spaatz, General and U.S. Army Air Forces Chief of Staff

07
DISCUSSION
ABOUT DISCUSSION
BY DIANA HADLEY

"Don't raise your voice, improve your argument."

—*Nelson Mandela*, South Africa President, Nobel Peace Prize Recipient

"The discussion itself is what most matters, the fact that we can reason together easily, with a blend of wit and seriousness, never descending into gossip or slander and always allowing room for alternative views."

—*Stephen Greenblatt*, The Swerve: How the World Became Modern

SCENARIO 1:

The members of a television talk show panel share opinions about events in the news. One member offers an outrageous remark. The audience claps and cheers. Another member of the panel reports that a tweet has just arrived with a counter to the remark; another section of the audience claps and cheers. The show continues as each person and tweet ratchets up the controversy, often the volume, and, the producers hope, the show's ratings.

SCENARIO 2:

Some high school students are upset with a new administrative policy. Rather than trying to meet with the principal to explain their frustration, they set up a Facebook page to mock the policy and take personal jabs at the administrators. While their initial concern is legitimate, the Facebook approach is disrespectful, though wildly popular among their peers, who add their own comments and escalate the conflict.

The two scenarios are different, but they have some common threads. In each case, people are sophisticated in the use of 21st century communication technology, but their message is a potential train wreck on a fast track.

In past years when people wrote letters to the editor by hand or on a manual typewriter to voice their opinions about an issue, the speed of the process created a built-in editing and cooling-off period. The fact that the mail might not go out for another 24 hours created a filter with time to look at the words again and reconsider their effect. The wait gave the writer a chance to ask some important questions.

- *Does this letter convey the message in the most effective way?*
- *Are the facts correct?*
- *Is the tone appropriate and conducive to making the point and/or solving the problem?*

Fast forward to 21st century communication that allows a knee-jerk reaction tweet or an instant reply to an article, and the filter system suffers or disappears completely. People have a greater opportunity to be heard and heard quickly, and that is good; but one downside is the opportunity to reply too hastily and be offensive at break-neck speed.

Another downside to a quick reply is the tendency to neglect thorough research and fact-checking. The Internet provides a wealth of information, but that information doesn't have to be right to be posted. It's not the encyclopedia of old but rather a garage sale of ideas that includes both treasures and junk. And what is the role of education in this dilemma? Unfortunately, at the very moment students need instruction to help them distinguish between the treasures and junk and to think on a faster, higher level, the national educational trend has turned to a rote-learning, standardized testing approach that stifles creativity and intellectual discourse.

David and I saw an example of this when we observed a college class that was struggling to discuss a topic. The professor divided the class into several smaller groups, generally an effective way to generate more ideas. As the small groups continued to struggle, one student complained to the professor about the activity and said, "Just tell us what we need to know. Don't make us think." In my experience such a comment would have been unusual to hear at the high school level a few years ago let alone college, but none of the students in the group seemed surprised by it, and some projected body language that indicated the speaker had addressed their frustration as well.

The connection of this situation with the study of nonviolence is multifaceted. Quick responses don't encourage students to evaluate sources and information thoroughly or to express themselves accurately. And the tendency to be confrontational doesn't help resolve conflicts.

Unfortunately, many students come from environments that approach conflict resolution with the same quick-fire, confrontational language they see in the media. In addition to talk shows and partisan, in-your-face cable news, programming like The Waltons and Father Knows Best has been replaced with shows that portray children responding to adults with wisecracks and disdain, not an approach that works well to solve problems outside of Television Land.

A nonviolence class is a perfect place to teach diplomatic, respectful communication. Many nonviolent leaders have perfected this kind of approach, and their words remain to be read or heard, pondered, and evaluated. It doesn't take many examples before students see the advantage of the approach and begin to adopt it in their own interactions within class discussions. Our goals are to provide information and a training ground for the positive exchange of opinions and ideas.

Our hope is that our students will embrace these skills as essential elements for their approach to all kinds of communication, and that they'll benefit long after they leave class and graduate to town council meetings and Thanksgiving dinners with in-laws.

08
GETTING THE CONTEXT RIGHT—TWO VOICES
DIANA HADLEY AND DAVID WEATHERSPOON

"Love casts out fear, but we have to get over the fear in order to get close enough to love them."

—*Dorothy Day, Social Activist, Co-Founder of Catholic Worker Movement*

DIANA: In journalism class, I like to use the Lincoln and Kennedy assassinations to show how communications have changed over time. It took weeks for the news of Lincoln's death to reach remote areas. Television and faster printing spread the detailed news about JFK instantly and let the country grieve collectively. It's a great comparison to show how people in 1865 and 1963 saw the news in different contexts.

DAVID: Yes, and there are much earlier examples. An incredible teacher in my seminary asked us to discuss the lyrics of Bob Marley and Lauryn Hill, and to inspect the main photo and caption on the front page of *The New York Times*. What was being said and not said? Only then did we start looking at ancient Biblical texts, to decipher what their first readers would have drawn from the language and stories of that time. We had as much trouble picturing what they were "getting," as they would have had understanding pop lyrics and the *Times*.

DIANA: Let's take more recent examples. How many of today's older generation grew up thinking the atomic bomb was necessary to end World War II or that the Berlin Wall fell thanks to a president's hard-nosed stance against Communism? The history...or context of each provides complicated stories. Similarly, the rise of Nazi Germany is more understandable if students know the context of how the World War I peace treaty and the depression of the 1930s affected Germany.

DAVID: It's all about context. Students in our nonviolence class are shocked to find that the history they've learned is often skewed by errors and omissions in context. It's a truism that victors write the history and show it in a light that justifies their actions. We make it a point to try to present all the facts, including those that that don't paint a particularly beautiful picture of actions by our country and its allies. We know we may never know all the truth, but we ought to discern it as well as we can.

DIANA: Getting context right also includes paying attention to humor and irreverence. Mark Twain wrote, "I love my country always and my government when it deserves it." In our class we've used the Stephen Colbert "truthiness" segments as a teaching tool, and also programs that juxtapose videos of contradictory statements from the same political parties, companies, and institutions, often from the same person.

DAVID: Context also involves not ignoring parts of the picture. Our students can quickly name major wars, but seldom the major nonviolent movements. They may know there was an American civil rights movement, but not have much understanding of it or its leaders, including people like Martin Luther King, Jr., Rosa Parks or Gandhi, on whose teachings much of the movement was based.

DIANA: And of course that movement feels as ancient to many students as David's Biblical scripts. The beauty of "commentators" like Colbert and Jon Stewart is that they quickly catch the attention of youthful listeners. And once subjects like Arab Spring are introduced to them, they're more likely to pursue research on their own.

DAVID: Let's not forget, though, that even when late-night TV gets them interested in current events, it doesn't often explain the roots of those events in the past. Most students haven't studied William Lloyd Garrison, Dorothy Day, James Lawson, or Nelson Mandela. Beyond the names of South Africa and apartheid, there's little knowledge of the struggle for human rights that took place there. Indian resistance to British rule is largely unknown, and so is Denmark's nonviolent resistance to the Nazis.

DIANA: Of course, but it's important to note that those late-night voices speak to students in their own voices. Jon Stewart interviewed a young woman leader of the Arab Spring movement. Our Midwestern students looked at her because she was their age and had learned about nonviolence in college. Class discussion focused on her knowledge, courage, and determination. It's empowering to our students to see people their age doing extraordinary things.

DAVID: And they can also compare the context of their own lives with that of young leaders elsewhere—and not just in foreign countries. When we discuss gun control, we divide our students into urban, suburban, and rural, and quickly discover that their feelings about guns largely reflect the context in which they were raised.

DIANA AND DAVID: And now, in unison, "Get the context right."

09
LEARNING FROM CLASSROOM VISITORS
BY DAVID WEATHERSPOON

"The great thing about social movements is everybody gets to be a part of them."

—Jim Wallis, Editor, *Sojourners*

People make a movement. Movements could never exist without the personalities, leadership, foresight, knowledge, and skill sets of those who carry their banners. Some of the most useful tools that Diana and I have found are the people we've invited to class to share their own stories of conflict resolution and their thoughts on nonviolent action. Later, we'll be sharing in detail the tremendous credibility and presence that Daniel Gates, a military veteran, offered as a student and peer of the nonviolence class. As much as anyone who has spoken to students, Daniel's reflections on the importance of the class and curriculum held great sway with the other students as well as with Diana and me. For his contributions, we'll always be grateful.

We've also been fortunate to have had campus guests who met with our nonviolence class. Marcus Borg, theologian and scholar, did a presentation on the teachings of Jesus that proved quite provocative for our students. He described the historical Jesus and illustrated how the methods of Jesus were subversive to Roman authority as well as to the religious leaders of the day. Jesus' actions stirred great unrest in the community, although Jesus himself always responded in a nonviolent way that circumvented the customary ways of dealing with malcontents in Roman society. He posed a real problem simply because he did the unexpected. Many of the students had never imagined the historical Jesus in this context.

Kevin Quigley, the executive director of the National Peace Corps Association when he visited the class, had an open discussion with the students. He posed an important question to them, asking, "What difference can you make in the world?" This conversation meshed well with the discussions the class had been having about the roles young men and women the age of our students were taking in major nonviolent movements like the American civil rights movement, the Arab Spring, and Occupy Wall Street. Students also had opportunities to discuss the benefits of the Peace Corps as they learned about the cultural preparation, including language development and acclimatization, that Peace Corps members experience. Quigley shared how the skills he gained in the Peace Corps translated to his current work. The students heard a particular fearlessness in Quigley's words and a curiosity to learn more.

Challenging the status quo and common assumptions is a major part of nonviolent resistance. Rabbi Steve Ballaban personified challenging such misperceptions. Ballaban spoke to the class about the incessant turmoil between Israelis and Palestinians. Instead of a defense of Israel's actions against the Palestinians, Ballaban was quick to critique the Israeli government and the violent suppression of Palestinian resistance. For the students to hear a rabbi outraged by Israeli settlements in Palestinian territory brought many questions to their minds. I think it helped them realize that they could be citizens of a country and still have major disagreements with those in power.

Ballaban offered his own path to resolving the conflict, saying that the Palestinians have more power than they realize. If they would simply refuse to work their day-to-day jobs in Israel and stop throwing rocks, it would bring the state of Israel to its knees in search of compromise, he said. But once again, he added, it would have to be a nonviolent resolution, because violence will only perpetuate the cycle of death and destruction shown nightly on television.

Ballaban was quick to discuss the media's control over the American cultural understanding of the Israeli/Palestinian crisis. He pointed out to the students that they currently receive a very narrow presentation of the facts due to Israel's lobbying of the media. Students would also learn more about the American Israel Public Affairs Committee (AIPAC) through resources that Diana and I use for class, but a personal critique from an insider like Ballaban was seen by students as a valuable contribution to their education.

Evelyn Hanneman was operations coordinator with the Baptist Peace Fellowship and specialized in conflict resolution when she visited our class. Even college students need a change of learning environments, so Evelyn took our students into a large open space, and directed them to divide up according to which animals most resembled their own conflict styles. One animal was very aggressive and loved to solve conflicts head on, while another ran at the very suggestion of the word.

In all, there were six style groupings, in which the students explored the positive and negative traits of their own styles. Afterwards, they had to consider whom they would need as an ally in the room in order to work through conflict. For instance, the rhinoceros might need a fox in order to compensate for the weaknesses of someone who likes to barrel in and charge through a problem. It was a great learning exercise that highlighted the thoughtfulness needed in conflict resolution, and how identifying the strengths and weaknesses of different styles could lead to a nonviolent and peaceful outcome where everyone wins. Students responded very well to this role playing, which can become a form of retained learning for real-world situations later.

Sometimes a very effective class visitor can be someone close at hand. One such person for us was a fellow faculty member, Edward Chikwana. A native of Africa, he challenged our students to say whether they considered America a violent country. The initial blank looks suggested that this thought had never occurred to many of them, especially those raised in protective middle- or upperclass surroundings. We asked Edward to comment on his experience, both as a student and speaker in the class. Here's what he wrote:

A SURPRISING CLASS
BY EDWARD CHIKWANA

One perk of being a faculty member at Franklin College is getting to take classes that you find interesting. Going to college in Zimbabwe, which follows the British educational model, I never had the opportunity to attend a liberal-arts college where I could learn about other areas besides my specialty in chemistry, so I have made it my goal to attend as many classes outside the sciences as I can. In Zimbabwe violence accompanies almost every election, so I was interested in nonviolence as a way of conflict resolution.

The class covered many good topics, but what I found most striking was the students' perception of violence/nonviolence in the United States. Given how many wars the U.S. has been involved in over the last 20 years, most of the students never saw this as a reflection on the nation's use of violence to resolve issues. I did understand their point of view, given that all these wars have been on foreign soil and thus the violence has not directly affected most of them in any way. The U.S. has taken the role of the world's policeman, making it very hard for the government to advocate nonviolence when it spends more money on the defense budget than on education. I believe the class structure and discussions allowed students to make up their own minds about the importance of nonviolence by providing them with the necessary tools to make informed decisions without trying to convert everyone into a peace activist.

Another surprising aspect of the class was the response to the discussions on gun ownership. Even after numerous discussions, I don't believe anyone in the class was moved to change his or her mind, because it seems everyone had very strong reasons to support their anti- or pro-guns views. I had also never looked at the gun issue as an urban vs. rural one; from the discussions I realized how guns represented something totally different, depending on whether you lived in rural Indiana, where hunting was part of the culture, or in the city where the word "gun" is so often followed by the word "violence," and is something to be feared. For those who support no change in current gun laws, guns and violence aren't always related; owning a gun (or more than one) has no bearing on whether you're a proponent of nonviolence or not.

What I found very interesting from the class was that even though Mahatma Gandhi honed his skills and started the whole nonviolence movement in South Africa, Africa as a continent has probably had the most instances of violent uprisings, including the recent ones in North Africa. The United States ends up getting involved in many of these situations, which is one reason I believe the class should be required for all students; they are the nation's future leaders, and this class gives them a good foundation in nonviolent conflict resolution.

The nature of the instructors' backgrounds—David Weatherspoon, a Baptist minister, and Diana Hadley, a Quaker —added a lot of value to the class. You could tell from the discussions that they didn't just teach nonviolence, they believed in it. Even though they both had strong religious reasons to advocate nonviolence, the class was never about religion, but rather about what we owe ourselves as part of the human race. As part of our social contract, we owe it to each other to value human life and use nonviolence as our default response to any conflict, personal or otherwise.

10
IMAGES
THAT RESONATE
BY DIANA HADLEY

"I have a dream that my four little children
will one day live in a nation where they
will not be judged by the color of their skin
but by the content of their character."

—Martin Luther King Jr., "I Have a Dream"

College students generally have some knowledge
of the American civil rights movement. They
know Martin Luther King Jr. played a leading role,
and most of them have seen video or read his
"I Have a Dream" speech.

Teachers are bound to incorporate their personal connections with a subject as they develop curriculum. I think that when the class is about nonviolence this personal connection increases. David and I bring different backgrounds to this process since we represent different generations and grew up in different regions of the country; but comparing our experiences often helps us find direction for the study units for our students, who have life experiences of their own and represent a different generation than either of us.

As impressive as Dr. King and his words were then and remain today, that movement was so much more. It's difficult to cover its magnitude within a high school history curriculum, and the fact that it draws attention to a less-than-flattering picture of many Americans makes it a challenge for textbook authors to revisit. It's also a challenge to do the movement justice in a one-semester college nonviolence course. The topic has many layers, and the full story should include all of them.

I grew up during the American civil rights movement. Although I was too young during part of it to remember many details, I still have vivid images in my memory of specific days. I remember a vacation to the South that introduced me to restrooms marked "Men," "Ladies," and "Colored." I remember news clips of police dogs intimidating young black people peacefully marching in protest. And I remember when a segregated high school won the Indiana state basketball championship, the first black school in the nation to win a state title.

I also remember that the people in my white rural community were frightened as the movement gathered strength. They were afraid the country would break out into extreme violence. That the United States didn't devolve into a civil war in the environment I remember from the 1950s and 1960s is amazing, and it's important that we study why it didn't.

Although television was still in its infancy and not many people carried movie cameras, images remain that help us connect the dots that led to change. And those images are unforgettable.

One treasure is a segment of the PBS series, *A Force More Powerful*, that shows the Nashville movement from the beginning when James Lawson taught non-violent strategies to college students. He used a variety of teaching techniques including role-play that required the students to act out verbal and physical abuse so they could practice nonviolent resistance. When they sat down at a real lunch counter where blacks were forbidden, they had a plan based on practice and the understanding of the discipline required for civil disobedience to be effective. All they needed at that point was courage.

Examples of that courage are preserved in a series of images on vintage film of polite, well-dressed college students being verbally mistreated and arrested just for sitting at a lunch counter. When I watched the black and white film for the first time decades later, it gave me chills. And that never changes. I feel the same awe each time I watch it, and our students (born decades later) are equally or more engaged because they see behavior that is undeniably not acceptable today—and they realize it was quite acceptable to a segment of the populace during that time in U.S. history.

Freedom Riders, a documentary produced more recently, provides another historical glimpse of the Civil Rights movement. Although it is too long to show during most classes, segments can be used with part of an Oprah show that paid tribute to the Freedom Riders on the 50th anniversary of the trip. The combination of the two creates a basic idea of the event and its aftermath. Although the Oprah tribute is good in its entirety, there is a special moment when a former KKK member who had attacked a student is added to the group to tell his story. He explains that after many years he visited the former student, Georgia Congressman John Lewis, to apologize. As he relates his story, he is obviously overwhelmed and anxious. And that's when John Lewis gently puts his hand on his former attacker's arm—a simple gesture that speaks volumes about forgiveness.

Lewis's reassurance is a touching example of how genuine victories in a nonviolent movement shouldn't include dancing in the end zone or cutting down nets. David and I can tell students they should be gracious if the movement succeeds, but John Lewis shows what "gracious" looks like, and the discussion that follows indicates that our students get it. Students conclude that the former KKK member still feels shame long after the event and his apology, and that Lewis appears to be a humble man who is comfortable in his own skin.

The layers of the civil rights story challenge the length of time the unit requires, because there were so many people and groups who need to be included. Like many nonviolent movements, the total success depended on those who were involved in small but significant ways in communities large and small across the country.

Ruby Bridges, who helped break the color barrier in New Orleans, became an icon of the early days of school integration, but many other parents risked physical harm to their children and economic hardship to their families by being the first to send their children to newly integrated schools in their communities.

Unsung heroes also included behind-the-scenes workers who did the detail work to organize demonstrations. "I Have a Dream" was a great speech, but it resonated because the Mall was filled with thousands of people who came to Washington, D.C., and they left the city intact, thanks to years of small steps, patience, and determination by many.

11
THE POWER
OF A PAPER CLIP
DAVID WEATHERSPOON AND DIANA HADLEY

" . . .they shall beat their swords into plowshares, and their spears into pruning hooks; nation shall not lift up sword against nation, neither shall they learn war any more." – *Isaiah 2:4*

Most people don't know what plows, salt and paper clips have in common. An old religious symbol of nonviolence is the plow. The Hebrew prophets Isaiah and Micah speak of a day when the choice weapons are transformed into plows and pruning hooks. It was a vision of ancient times when there would no longer be a need for weaponry designed for the purpose of killing another person. Instead, these instruments of death and destruction would be converted into the chief tools of life and creation, the plow and the pruning hook. Many civilizations lived in constant fear of overthrow and plunder from rival nations. To dream of a day when all could have their own plot of land to till and garden without threat of others was the ray of hope many longed to realize.

The plow maintained its symbol of peace and nonviolence as the Maori people under the leadership of Te Whiti decided to take back the land that had been stolen from them not by violence but by plows. The Maori began to plow the fields that they had once owned. The new landowners did not know what to do with this nonviolent protest. It is hard to justify the killing and domination of someone who is simply tilling the land. The protest helped preserve a remnant of the Maori people in New Zealand who would have otherwise been wiped off the earth if they had met the hostility they had received with further violence

Although students have heard of Gandhi and maybe his march to sea, they may not realize the significance of a handful of salt. However, media savy students soon see the powerful symbolism of the action when Gandhi defies unjust British laws against India's production of its own resource. They can find similarities to current unjust government policies throughout the world and within their own borders.

Asked to name other peace symbols students might think of the circular art that Gerald Holtom designed to represent the British nuclear disarmament movement in 1958. Fewer will know that the center lines represent semaphore signals for the letters "N" and 'D' for "nuclear disarmament," but many will associate the icon with antiwar activists in later movements. Although this surprises me, some of our students associate it with "hippies" who protested during the Vietnam era. Still others know it as a popular design for jewelry, shirts and accessories of 21st Century fashion.

Because students are familiar with it, Holtom's peace symbol is a great example for a study about the effect and evolution of an artistic image that represents a peace movement. It is also a good example for class because it has sent both positive and negative visual messages in a variety of circumstances over a period of decades.

Another great example of an effective symbol is the title of a middle school project that expanded to a global lesson, the paper clip.

Johan Vaaler, a Norwegian inventor with a degree in electronics, science and mathematics, invented the paper clip in 1899. Although others may have created something similar, he was the first to patent it in Germany and then the United States since Norway didn't provide patents.

When Germany occupied Norway from 1940-1945, Norwegians wore a paper clip on their collar or cuff as a symbol of solidarity for each other and those who were persecuted.

That information entered into a Whitwell, Tennessee, middle school classroom discussion when students studied the Holocaust in 1999. One student said he couldn't imagine the loss of six million lives because he couldn't imagine six million of anything. As students and their teachers tried to think of something a poor Appalachian school system could afford to collect six million of, another student found the link to paper clips and Jewish persecution.

"Paper Clips," a documentary produced in 2003, tells the story of a school project that went global. Its 84-minute running time allows for a complete showing and discussion in two classes. The film won some film festival awards, and it isn't an exaggeration to say that our students love this film.

They see a small community become a global news story as the Whitwell students begin to contact celebrities and ask them for paper clip donations to represent the six million Jewish lives that were lost during the Holocaust. When two German journalists see their story on a website, they write about the project and visit the school. Their reporting leads to a network nightly news story that breaks the lull in the collection process eventually bringing in 27 million papers clips, most in individual letters, to a community of 1,600 people and a small post office that couldn't handle the influx.

The paper clips project was impressive on many levels, but one special result was the participation and education of an entire community and eventually many people throughout the country.

12
WORDS TO THE WISE
BY DAVID WEATHERSPOON

"There is something about words. In expert hands, manipulated deftly, they take you prisoner. Wind themselves around your limbs like spider silk, and when you are so enthralled you cannot move, they pierce your skin, enter your blood, numb your thoughts. Inside you they work their magic."

— *Diane Setterfield, The Thirteenth Tale*

"But if thought corrupts language, language can also corrupt thought."

—*George Orwell, 1984*

Communication is one of the most important elements in maintaining a healthy society. It is also one of the most difficult.

Colloquial language and interpretation can lead to much misunderstanding even in the best of circumstances. However, there are times when misunderstanding is the desired goal of the one in power who is delivering the message. If mass audiences misunderstand the message, they are often inclined either to chase another rabbit or to sit quietly on the side and not ask too many questions. The use of language greatly influences the response of the masses.

In recent years, the word "reform" has been used by both major political parties to introduce legislation that each argues will be good for the country. Reform is a concept that most people can rally behind. Most people want reform in one way or another, but the details that make up a particular kind of reform vary greatly. The media are filled with messages of education reform, tax reform, gun reform, and immigration reform. However, what is meant when one party says, "gun reform," is often very different from what the opposing party means. The word "reform" is very useful these days in gaining support for a particular agenda without needing to provide too many details about what one side means by the term.

Emotionally charged words are often used to build blind support. Words such as "freedom" and "patriotic" are employed to squelch opposition. In much the same way as wearing a flag pin when running for office, these words can be used to reassure the mass audience of one's loyalty and identity in the national political picture, as well as to stake a claim to the "right" side of the debate. Thus, the opposition is deemed as "unpatriotic" or as imposing demands that take away people's freedoms. These emotional appeals rarely have much substance; they are simply meant to persuade the audience of who is and is not to be trusted with power.

This emotional tactic is very effective. One of the greatest emotional appeals of the early 21st Century used claims of "freedom" and "democracy" in an attempt to gain support for the invasion of Iraq. The phrase, "weapons of mass destruction," became instrumental in a calculated media blitz to create a national fervor for war. Despite substantial and convincing evidence to the contrary from the United Nations' inspection teams, the White House staff appeared on every major media outlet trumpeting the presence of WMDs at the fingertips of Saddam Hussein. He was deemed an "imminent threat." It was not if but when he would unleash his arsenal of biological and chemical weapons, the argument ran, and if our country did not act, we would be on the wrong side of history. The frenzy culminated in the March 2003 invasion of Iraq despite considerable resistance within the United States. Much of this resistance was labeled "unpatriotic" in an attempt to silence the voices of those daring to raise questions and to isolate them as outsiders or even traitors.

What exactly is a weapon of mass destruction? Is it limited to biological, chemical, and nuclear weapons, or could the term include weapons like the AK-47? Certainly it's one of the most common assault weapons worldwide, with many deaths attributed to it. Or could the term WMD include the weapons used by Adam Lanza (Bushmaster AR-15 and two handguns, a Glock 10 mm and Sig Sauer 9 mm) in the Sandy Hook school shooting at Newtown, Conn., which left 28 people including 20 children dead? Certainly, it could be argued that the Newtown incident was mass destruction through the use of powerful weapons in the wrong hands.

Diana and I begin class with a little exercise that illustrates the power of language. We give a brief pre-test. One of the phrases on this pre-test is "collateral damage," which we ask the students to define. Afterwards, we offer a news bulletin: "A terrorist in Fallujah was killed today. There was collateral damage." The students are asked if that story is okay with them. Usually, few if any have a problem with it. We then share the same story worded differently: "A terrorist in Fallujah was killed today. Among those also killed were an innocent mother and her two children." We then ask the students their response. Invariably, none of the students are okay with this version. Then the students discuss the term "collateral damage" and conclude that it sanitizes the violence so that it seems acceptable.

13
ANALYZING MEDIA MESSAGES
BY DIANA HADLEY

"The difference between the right word
and the almost right word is the difference
between lightning and a lightning bug."

—Mark Twain, Author, Humorist

Twenty-first Century students tend to be technically
savvy with social media and numerous platforms of
communication. They can design websites, find information they want
from a multitude of sources and communicate with almost anyone anywhere.
But just because they can manipulate the technology doesn't mean they
communicate effectively . . . or responsibly. And that problem provides another
area that a nonviolence class can address.

For example, as students access information for class assignments, they can observe the feedback readers add at the end of articles and blogs and evaluate its accuracy and objectivity. Given the opportunity, students become adept at analyzing the motives and prejudices of the responses. Even though many negative responses don't contribute positively to an issue, they do provide a baseline that students who aren't emotionally involved in the topic can use as they learn to respond effectively to other issues.

Educators who promote "media literacy" have added an important concept to the word "literacy." Not only must students be able to read, they need to be able to detect the nuance and back story of what they read.

David has already given some examples of emotionally charged words and deliberate attempts to misdirect an issue by calling it something it isn't. Once that has been explained, students are pretty quick to identify other examples within the context of the class. Consider the following questions about a world issue:

- *Are "neighborhoods" the same thing as "settlements" when journalists talk about disputed areas in Palestine?*
- *Are the journalists intentionally selecting certain words to slant the way the story is perceived?*
- *Could the journalists be using press releases from one side or the other without carefully considering the content or context?*
- *Is it possible the journalists just don't know enough about the conflict to make the most appropriate or accurate vocabulary choices?*

Just talking about the possibilities above can generate good class discussion. Creating some healthy skepticism adds dimension to the learning process that should later serve the students well when they participate in discussion or debate about an issue, whether they're defending or challenging their viewpoints. After learning to analyze the language they see and hear, they're more likely to choose their own words with the precision that promotes their points most effectively.

My high school students loved the story of Koko the gorilla who learned sign language. Koko began to create compound words, one of which was the combined signs for "toilet" and "head," which she called her trainer when she was mad at her. Name-calling seems to be a natural evolution of language whether the communicator is a gorilla who signs or a nursery school class, but it's a primitive tool that doesn't elevate discussion to an intellectual level. The hope is that with education people will evolve to more reasonable and less contemptuous dialogue that helps solve problems.

Once students appreciate the effect of the right word or words, it's important to add the effect of tone. The nonviolence class is a perfect place to find examples of people who can elevate intense, passionate discussion beyond name-calling and hostility. While many television shows and movies depict the response to a loud or aggressive speech as louder and more aggressive (often leading to physical violence), nonviolent activists disarm their loud or disagreeable opponents with a quiet response. This gives the receiver a considerable amount of power over the situation since either response often creates more of the same.

As Gandhi replies quietly and respectfully to his adversaries in South Africa and India, they seem to be led if not transformed to do the same. When television reporters question Dr. Martin Luther King Jr. about the use of marches and demonstrations during the civil rights movement, he calmly explains the rationale for drama to educate and inform. Students watch the historic videos or movies of these real events and are moved by the power of calm reason and honesty. David and I don't include test questions that ask which of the approaches is right. Our students' responses to the examples are all the feedback we need to know that they been impressed by the power of calm reason.

14
THE WAKE-UP CALL OF TRAVELING
BY DAVID WEATHERSPOON

"Travel is fatal to prejudice, bigotry, and narrow-mindedness, and many of our people need it sorely on these accounts. Broad, wholesome, charitable views of men and things cannot be acquired by vegetating in one little corner of the earth all one's lifetime."

—*Mark Twain,* *"The Innocents Abroad/Roughing It"*

Mabel invited a group of us into her home. We had been working for the past couple of days trying to clean up the debris left around her place by Hurricane Katrina.

Mabel had lived here most of her life. She had experienced the effects of previous hurricanes, but these weren't like Katrina. Despite all the devastation to her neighborhood and her own home, Mabel was still keeping up her spirits and doing what she loved. Most of our group had never experienced a real praline before that day. She pulled out a whole tray that she had baked especially for the volunteers who had helped her through debris removal and had simply sat with her as she shared her stories.

The listening ear is often one of the most hospitable gifts a person can offer. In turn, Mabel was demonstrating true southern hospitality as she invited all of us to partake of one of her special treats. The gesture clearly moved several students. They had come to the Gulf Coast on their spring break to help and offer their resources, and yet they were the ones being welcomed and shown hospitality.

One of the gifts of my work is the ability to lead students on educational, mission, and service endeavors. Before going on these transformational opportunities, there's an orientation meant to prepare students to be learners and work alongside people in whatever context they find themselves. I emphasize that the work will be a drop in the bucket of the need that exists, but these drops are necessary. The real major change will come in the lives of those who are participating. They are removed from their own contexts and familiar routines. The blinders from their daily lives are set aside; they can see the world in new and fresh ways when they don't know what to expect. The hope is they'll return home and be able not only to see the daily needs around them, but also to use the tools they've discovered on these trips to make a positive difference in their communities.

The trips vary in initiatives. One opportunity may be a cultural immersion experience. Another may meet a particular need, like the Katrina relief trip or similar efforts to assist those affected by the Tuscaloosa tornado. There can also be an educational advocacy and service focus from which students learn about ways they can systematically help in social justice endeavors.

 Abyssinian Baptist Church in New York City is the oldest African-American church in the country, dating back to 1804. The theologian Dietrich Bonhoeffer would occasionally attend the church because he was moved by its social justice efforts. When our group visited, they heard how the church had been proactive in the abolition and civil rights movements, and how it was considering challenging the city of New York for stopping and arresting African-Americans at rates far exceeding their percentage in the population. The person giving us the tour suggested that 80 percent of the police stops in New York were people of color whereas the African-American population was only about 34 percent of the total.

That evening, during small-group debriefing sessions, some students made insightful observations. One young man said he hadn't realized the extent of racism in today's society. Another student was impressed by the continuing effort of this particular church as it strives to root out the various injustices afflicting society. Through listening to their reflections about the day, it was clear that these young men and women were beginning to tap into the ways that they could be agents of positive change in the world. They were realizing they could be transformers.

In Washington, D.C., there is a place called Christ House, which sprang from the Church of the Savior as a way to prevent people from being turned away from hospitals with only nominal care. The facility works to provide a place where the uninsured homeless can find real care for a variety of ailments. It is a holy place. After hearing about this facility and the people there, Leslie, one of the students on the trip, said it could be a place where she would later intern. She wasn't able to go to Christ House on the day our group visited because she was at another D.C. location. But the stories her peers shared with her about their visit piqued her interest. They told her about the dignity and humanity with which every person was treated. They spoke about the doctors and other care providers who lived in residence with many of the formerly homeless, at Christ House and a transitional housing facility. Leslie realized this was the kind of place that practiced justice, and she wanted to be part of that story.

Such trips are important because they create a mindset that understands how people can make a difference if they are educated to do so. Nothing combats violence better than education and participation in real, tangible forms of advocacy and justice. The people who emerge from such encounters realize that people are people, and that most simply need a helping hand along the way for a better outcome. Preventing racism, assisting people out of poverty and homelessness, and practicing hospitality are all missions of nonviolence. They are also part of what it means to be a healthy society.

15
OH, THE PLACES YOU SHOULD GO!
BY DIANA HADLEY

"Experience, travel—these are an education in themselves."—*Euripides, Greek Author*

"Perhaps travel cannot prevent bigotry, but by demonstrating that all peoples cry, laugh, eat, worry, and die, it can introduce the idea that if we try and understand each other, we may even become friends."—*Maya Angelou, Poet, Activist*

The Quaker influence of my heritage is balanced with my dad's side of the family. Dad and two of his brothers served in World War II. Another of my uncles and multiple cousins have served the U.S. military and in a variety of capacities in Korea, Vietnam, Germany, Iraq, and Afghanistan. The sacrifices they and their families have made place them in a group that I, like most people, respect.

I know families who avoid subjects that cause conflict at holiday dinners. I like to think my relatives do that, but I don't remember many discussions about the military at our reunions—maybe because the family members in the military outnumbered the Quakers exponentially.

One of my most serious discussions with an uncle happened quite by accident when I met several relatives at a restaurant for lunch a few years ago. In the haphazard selection of seats around the table, my Uncle Gene and I ended up sitting next to each other. I knew at once I'd be entertained over the next hour because he had a great sense of humor.

However, at some point our conversation turned to my teaching career. Suddenly, he looked very serious and told me to make sure my students traveled so they would meet people from other places, realize they had much in common, and not want to kill them. I was struck because this retired Marine had spent a lifetime serving his country all over the world, but had never shared a single moment of this experience or his reflections about it with me.

Even though I look back and wish I had asked more questions, his sincere tip seemed totally sufficient at the time, and I filed it away in the part of my brain that stores profound thoughts until later.

The comment may not have seemed profound at that moment because I have always been a proponent of travel as an important educational tool. For many years I took journalism students to Chicago to visit the *Chicago Tribune*. The obvious objective was to see how a large city newspaper operates, but my colleagues and I also wanted students to experience the culture of a big city:

its infrastructure, transportation, commercial systems, and a more diverse population than that of the small suburban town where they lived. We prepped them with background about the places they would visit and instructions to observe but not stare at people who were different from them.

It's easy to tell people not to stare—harder for them to resist doing just that in a new environment. During one of the Chicago trips a woman traveling on a city bus with my group moved to a seat in front of me, the obvious leader of the group, and said, "Your kids are staring at me. Haven't they ever seen black people?" Staring—exactly what we had told them not to do! I apologized and explained that we were from a small town where everyone looked alike and had come to Chicago so the students could learn about other people and places.

She said, "Okay then. I'm going to tell them about us." And then she transitioned from someone who was insulted to a guest speaker. She stood in the aisle of the bus and explained to my students that many people in large cities don't have cars and rely on public transportation. She described the city's jobs and schools. As she taught my students in a way I could not, I was gratified by the goodness of strangers . . . but I still gave my kids a look that said, "This is turning out okay, but stop staring at people."

We all learn when we step away from the classroom and into the rest of world. And "the rest of the world" can be relatively nearby. I have taken the nonviolence class to the Indianapolis Peace Learning Center a number of times to let them observe fourth-grade classes as the children spend a day learning about nonviolent leaders and hands-on nonviolent strategies. In addition to hearing the lessons themselves, it's a great opportunity for my class to compare and contrast different elementary schools and the challenges they face with their students.

Some of the college students just watch, but others spontaneously begin to participate. That participation creates the special sauce that validates the experience for everyone.

16
VIOLENCE SELLS
BY DIANA HADLEY

"Peace cannot be kept by force.
It can only be achieved by understanding."

—*Albert Einstein,* Theoretical Physicist

Nagging concerns about the violence that permeates movies, television, and video games have not kept most people from shelling out significant sums of money to buy the games or increase the effect of a movie by paying extra to see it in 3-D on a large screen in a theater.

My husband and I have been movie fans for decades. We have seen hundreds of movies including many with violent themes that were troubling. Yet I have walked out of only one movie before it ended to protest over-the-top violence. I recently attended a movie I expected to dislike, rationalizing that I couldn't criticize anything I hadn't seen. Now I can criticize it, but I am hardly in a position to persuade others not to see it since I had read the reviews and knew it would be violent. What a conundrum.

This admission is the basis of my approach to class discussions about topics centering on violent media that I might be tempted to judge. I may not like it, but I'm not afraid the violence I see in a movie is going to transform me into a violent or even a more aggressive or desensitized person. My students feel the same way about themselves. I make it clear that I accept the fact they are mature, well-adjusted people who can separate a video game from reality.

However, I expand the discussion to see if they feel the violence is also appropriate for a younger brother, sister, niece, or nephew who may not have the maturity to compartmentalize what they experience and separate it from reality. This new scenario provides a different perspective that leads some of them to share concerns and offer remedies ranging from parental responsibility, to ratings and sometimes even censorship.

They agree that people mature at different rates, and they find it difficult to decide on the perfect age for "mature viewing" designations. Violence is often less of a factor in their ratings discussion than sexual issues or profanity.

In general, people oppose "Big Brother" regulation and censorship in theory; and the courts agree. A 2011 Supreme Court decision struck down a California case involving sales of violent games to minors.

Even James Steyer, CEO and founder of Common Sense Media, believes people accept violence as part of life because they have become numb to it after being exposed to violence so often. Yet he, too, is against a heavy hand. The organization's motto is "Sanity, Not Censorship," and Steyer suggests better selectivity as the answer. A class about nonviolence helps establish talking points for selectivity.

Some researchers are trying to prove a connection between violent media and tragedies such as Newtown in which Adam Lanza, the young man who killed 20 children and six staff members, had spent a great deal of time playing violent video games. But until there is more definitive information regarding causation vs. correlation of media violence and actual violence, class discussion about it will be lively but not conclusive.

That does not make the topic a waste of time. Any discussion that leads students to analyze the status quo and their role in it is worthwhile.

It's important to point out that when people attend a movie or buy a video game their dollars are "votes" that encourage producers to make more of that genre of entertainment. Sometimes most of the choices are violent. And that leads to a discussion of the economics of entertainment violence.

Violence in the media provides several angles for student presentations. Leading students to do research that interests them is key. They find the numbers for national sales for video games and the time people spend playing them. As they compile the information, they are able to evaluate the influence of this kind of entertainment within their own lives. Understanding the role that violence plays in their lives is a revelation that leads to new awareness and choice.

As more people develop awareness and become more selective with their choices change is possible. That change is already obvious within many film festivals. The Heartland Film Festival's theme is "Truly moving motion pictures that celebrate the power of the human spirit." Launched in Indianapolis in 1992, Heartland has become one of the most popular independent film festivals in the country. The annual event demonstrates the positive potential of the movies. Attendance increased by 13 percent from 2012 to 2013 with 24,000 people attending during the 10-day screenings. The total of 1,521 film submissions broke the previous record of 1,292 in 2012. Seventy-six countries submitted films with 120 filmmakers attending from 10 countries. While the numbers don't compete with feature films that benefit from millions of marketing dollars, they do indicate an increasing interest in other choices.

THE PEACE CLASS *A study of effective cheek-turning, neighbor-loving and sword-to-plowshare conversion*

17
TALKING ABOUT GUNS
DIANA HADLEY AND DAVID WEATHERSPOON

"A weapon is an enemy even to its owner."

—Turkish Proverb

David and I decided we needed to think of a way to talk about guns. How could we help students understand the origins of different gun cultures and philosophies? Although we had impressive statistics and essays representing multiple sides of the gun debate, we decided we would try to discover differences within a class that seemed to have little diversity. Not knowing for sure what we would find, we divided the class into rural, suburban, and urban groups according to where the students grew up. Then we asked them to describe their personal association with guns.

Our first speakers represented the rural contingent. Their stories were similar, honest, and confident. Some had always known guns, and they were very comfortable with them. They believed they had been taught safe gun use, and they didn't share any negative incidents with guns. Some said they worried that a new president would limit their access to guns, so their families had purchased more.

Brandon, typically vocal and well-liked by his classmates, described deer hunting and the dressing of venison with impressive details. Some of his classmates were nodding in agreement with his points. They didn't seem to notice the faces that indicated others were listening to the description of a culture as unusual to them as that of a foreign country.

A couple of suburban students followed the rural speakers. They said their families had a gun or guns for hunting or protection. One joked that his parents had a gun that was in a safe, so an intruder would have to be patient and wait for them to work the combination before they sprang into action to protect the home and family.

Could anyone speak about guns in an urban environment? Speaking from the front of the room, Brittany shared a distinctly stated sentence: "We have guns, but we don't hunt."

There was silence as her classmates realized she had added an element to the discussion that changed the dynamic. She then described with deft, first-hand knowledge a neighborhood, her neighborhood, where kids had guns to protect themselves or intimidate other kids their age in a culture that experienced frequent personal violence.

In the discussion that followed, members of the class helped each other understand that they had some very different attitudes about guns due to very different life circumstances, which they didn't control and took for granted as the status quo.

A couple of students stayed after class to continue the conversation. One of them thanked us for initiating the discussion.

After the last few students left, David and I concluded that we had lucked into a unique class moment. We've continued to use this strategy in other classes, and each time there are fascinating personal stories that describe unforgettable and often life-changing links between people and guns. Some of those stories are recounted by David below.

***

The dynamics in the room could not have been much more varied or more opportune for a lively gun-control discussion during the second year that Diana and I led the debate.

As we had done the previous year, we had students divide themselves into groups of rural, suburban, and urban. Once again, the rural students proved to be much more in favor of gun ownership, with the urban students more opposed and the suburban students a bit more ambivalent. Debate about how many guns one should be allowed to own and what types of guns and ammo should be used ensued. However, the stories that some students brought to the conversation that day were remarkable and trumped any lesson plan that Diana and I could have dreamed of preparing.

Kyle shared that he had no problem with guns and loved to hunt. He had grown up on a farm and had long since learned how to operate a firearm. In his mind, restrictions on guns were basically a bad idea. But Kyle did have a bit of a surprise for the class. He lifted his shirt and showed the scar on his side where he had been shot by someone who had misused a gun while they were hunting together. The professors were as stunned as anyone in the class. For some students, and perhaps even for Kyle, the scar was a badge of pride that he could use as a show-and-tell moment.

After a number of rural and some suburban students shared their comfort with guns (several said they owned multiple guns), Brittany could not contain herself any longer. She had a look of sheer horror on her face as she spoke about how frightened she was of guns and how astonished that so many of her peers owned not one but multiple weapons. This discovery terrified her. Brittany had been an elementary student in Columbine, Colorado, when her town had been devastated by a shooting spree at the high school led by two troubled teen-agers. She could not see anything good coming from civilians owning and possessing guns.

Samantha then described her father, a policeman. Sam said that her dad tried his best never to pull his weapon from his holster. He had told Sam that the second the gun is pulled everything gets more tense and deadly. "It's much easier," he said, "to talk a perpetrator down if you keep your gun in the holster." Pulling the gun only heightens the chances that a shootout will occur. Therefore, he wants to defuse situations as much as possible without using his firearm.

Normally, Adam was quiet in class and always polite, but this time he couldn't be silent. Adam said that he grew up in a tough neighborhood of his city. Guns had been around his entire life, but they had brought him nothing but pain. Four of Adam's close friends had been killed in separate shootings. His voice had a slight tremor to it that comes with speaking hard truths that touch the core of one's being. Adam had made it out of the neighborhood while many others had not. He now lived with the guilt and the relief that come from being a survivor.

It was another dynamic learning experience that both challenged us and helped us understand one another better. The stories shared that day brought to life the complexity of gun control. Certainly, the weighty issue had not been resolved, but it had been contextualized in a way that helped us all see and understand one another a little better.

18
WAR IS NOT A VIDEO GAME

BY DAVID WEATHERSPOON

"I object to violence because when it appears to do good, the good is only temporary; the evil it does is permanent."

—*Mahatma Gandhi, 20th Century Peace Activist*

I was in high school during the first war in Iraq. I remember watching the evening news and being mesmerized by the video of air raids on Iraqi forces. At the time, I viewed it proudly; the U.S. army was crushing Saddam's forces. It reminded me of the video games that I had played. There was very little thought about the loss of human life; it was watching power in action, and it was addictive. I couldn't turn away when these scenes appeared on the screen.

After the first war in Iraq, video games did begin to dramatically improve their realistic feel. Ultimately, *Gears of War, Soldier of Fortune,* and *Call of Duty,* to name a few, have nearly perfected the art of making a game seem real. Studies are being done to determine the effect that such games have on people who play them. Do they desensitize some people to violence? Are some people predisposed to overlook atrocities of war if they find enjoyment and entertainment in games that mimic real warfare? These are questions that we raise with our students. Students will admit that they enjoy playing some of these games, and although many say the games have had little to no impact on their own lives, they do often acknowledge that the realistic violence could be problematic for some people who play these games.

The games are so realistic that some have been used as simulation standards for real-life weapons and preparing soldiers for combat. Realistic weaponry is demanded of products being used in games. Is the gaming industry a recruiting and training strategy for actual military operations?

Post-traumatic stress disorder has been associated with drone operators stationed at locations in the United States. Thousands of miles removed from Afghanistan, Yemen, and Pakistan, these drone operators patrol the skies of these countries and are charged with initiating strikes on "high value targets." Unfortunately, much collateral damage has been reported from missed targets or among innocents near the targets. The result has left deep wounds not only in the countries targeted but also in the persons thousands of miles away manipulating the joystick controlling the drone.

War is not a video game. Real people die when attacked whether in hand-to-hand combat or remote strikes controlled from afar. The clandestine nature of the drones provides good questions for class.

- *Who is responsible for determining the likelihood of success of a particular strike?*
- *What are the risks that are considered acceptable in launching a drone attack?*
- *Who provides the checks and balances for these tactics?*
- *Who else has drone capability?*
- *Who decides who gets to use such capability and who does not?*

I admit I am troubled by these questions. I am reminded of Jesus' teaching that those who live by the sword shall die by the sword. Violence tends to lead to more violence. Only acts of nonviolence create a break in the cycle of death that allows transformation to happen. Collateral damage often results in new enemies with vendettas of vengeance that were not present before. No joy or entertainment should result from the operation of these devices. Yes, these are powerful weapons that are mesmerizing in their abilities and often precision, but they are also leaving many human beings either dead or picking up the pieces of their shattered lives.

War is not a video game.

19
THE 'JUST' WAR
BY DAVID WEATHERSPOON

"The guns and the bombs, the rockets and the warships, are all symbols of human failure."

—Lyndon B. Johnson, U.S. President

With the rare exception of an occasional religion major, few students have a clue about the inception of the "just war" theory. Their education up to this point has spent little time questioning the existence of war. Instead, it has dealt mostly with the stories told by the victors in various conflicts. Most students believe that war is simply an accepted phenomenon that has occurred since the beginning of time, and that not much can be done to thwart its inevitable cycle. They agree that it's horrific, but also a "natural" part of human nature and our history.

Still, people throughout history have clearly been at least bothered by the incessant presence of war. Early Christians were known to flee all forms of war, often refusing to fight even though they might be executed for that refusal. Some Christians were enlisted against their will and still would not wield a sword in combat because they believed it was a sin to kill another human being regardless of the reason.

As Christianity became the state religion under Constantine, a very shrewd emperor, Christianity took quite a twist. The cross became emblazoned upon the shields of the armies, and the soldiers of Rome began to fight in the name of Rome and of Christ. Still, the thought of killing another was problematic for many in the Christian church.

With the move of the Roman world to Christendom, the empire needed followers to fight for it. Along came Augustine, one of the most revered figures in all of church history. He set about writing the still-popular formula for waging a just war. Indeed, in a few strokes of his pen, the issue of military combat was resolved in the minds of most Christians for centuries to come. Those who dared challenge Augustine and his just war ideology were largely silenced. Crusades and other "holy" wars could now be unleashed. Terms such as "malacide" were coined to suggest that one was not killing another human being, which would have been homicide (murder). Instead, it meant the killing of a bad or non-human person, which could be considered acceptable.

The "conventions" of The Hague and Geneva expanded on the work of Augustine. They outlined rules of engagement in order to determine when a sovereign nation can declare war upon another sovereign nation. Some basic tenants of "just-war" theory include: war must be a last resort after all nonviolent options are exhausted; the reason for the war must be to redress rights actually violated or to defend against demands backed by force; the war must be openly and legally declared by a lawful government with a reasonable chance of winning; the military must try to distinguish between combatants and noncombatants, thus insuring that civilians are never purposely killed;

the force used must be proportional, meaning the evil done is less than the evil that would continue without war; and humiliation must never be the goal of the victor.

Such guidelines for conducting a war are fanciful at best. Each of these statutes has been broken in the declaring of wars throughout history. Rhetoric has been used to justify the aggressor's actions, and platitudes have been offered in response to the accusations of failing the just war criteria. Prior to the U.S. invasion of Iraq in 2003, former President Carter wrote a commentary for *The New York Times* (March 9, 2003) about the administration's lack of attention to the supposed code of war as it sought to invade Iraq without any real evidence to support its claims.

Let me be clear. War is never just. Quakers, Mennonites, Anabaptists, and a few other pacifist groups have mostly been the champions of this truth. The guidelines for a just war almost always become mere suggestions for a nation wishing to physically impose its will upon another. Civilians of all nations involved are invariably victimized by war. It is usually the sons and daughters of those with little wealth who are selected to bear the arms, to lose their limbs or lives, and to suffer post-traumatic stress disorder. It would be interesting to interview the current Congress and ask them how many children they have lost in battle.

Civilian casualties were more common in the wars of the last century than at any other time in history. This is one of the chief violations of just war doctrine. But the doctrine is needed by those in power to justify their own political agendas.

20
JUST FOLLOWING ORDERS
BY DAVID WEATHERSPOON

"Students must have initiative; they should not be mere imitators. They must learn to think and act for themselves—and be free."

—Cesar Chavez, Labor Activist, Co-founder of United Farm Workers

National Public Radio reported a story about cities that are trying to relocate homeless persons to less visible areas. The story told how a pastor in Raleigh, N.C., was threatened with arrest by a police officer if he did not leave a park where he was feeding the homeless.

The goal, supported by a city ordinance, was to remove resources from a population deemed undesirable, which the city wanted to move out of view—as though that would be a solution. The officer was also complicit in preventing the pastor and the church from the free exercise of their First Amendment rights, including the religious command given them to feed the hungry. I am fairly certain this doesn't mean just the hungry who are located where the city wants them to be.

On many occasions, civilians have lost their lives in war zones, either during combat in places like Vietnam, Iraq, and Afghanistan, or in drone warfare. In both kinds of cases, the officers and soldiers responsible have used the defense that they were, "just following orders." But isn't it more appropriate to refuse to follow an unjust order than it is to comply with the pressure of an authority figure?

Stanley Milgram conducted the famous Milgram study in 1963. In the experiment, volunteers administered a supposed electric shock to a "learner" who acted out his supposed pain. The voltage would then be increased and the shock repeated. The results were stunning; nearly 80 percent of the volunteers continued to administer increasing "pain" because they were just following orders. Following the Holocaust, many German soldiers claimed they carried out their horrific acts for the same reason—"just following orders."

Such a simplistic response to complex problems rings hollow. However, the evidence suggests that a majority of people are susceptible to coercive orders given by authority figures even when it goes against their better judgment. The challenge then is to teach people and especially our students how to critically analyze directives by authorities and decide whether or not the order should be followed, ignored, or confronted and challenged.

I wonder if the policeman in the Raleigh case ever questioned whether he should follow the city ordinance. My guess is that the church's First Amendment rights never crossed his mind, but when the act of feeding a hungry person is considered criminal, we need to have people who immediately begin to question the validity of such an ordinance. Diana and I have a major responsibility to teach students to move beyond mere "followership" and consider their role as responsible and informed citizens.

21
MILITARY DOLLARS AND SENSE
BY DIANA HADLEY

"Every gun that is made, every warship launched, every rocket fired, signifies in the final sense a theft from those who hunger and are not fed, those who are cold and are not clothed. This world in arms is not spending money alone. It is spending the sweat of its laborers, the genius of its scientists, the hopes of its children."

—Dwight D. Eisenhower, Five-Star General & U.S. President

No passes. The person who studies nonviolence but disregards math or economics as "not my thing" must learn to understand the numbers that affect peace efforts.

The study of nonviolence may be placed within the liberal arts section of the curriculum, but its math components provide statistics that need to be considered, not just by elected officials who create policies and prioritize programs that generate the country's bills but also by every engaged citizen.

In addition to the effective use of boycotts and strikes to provide economic pressure to counter violence or social injustice, students should have the opportunity to study the math of government budgets and analyze their overall significance regarding the best interests of the country. Although the figures are complicated and may vary from source to source, some estimates show percentages like the following for the United States budget for one year:

Government	6%
Education	6%
Veterans Benefits	5.5%
Housing and Community	5.5%
Health	5%
International Affairs	4%
Energy and Environment	3%
Science	2.5%
Labor	2.5%
Transportation	2%
Food and Agriculture	1%
Military*	57%

Military includes Department of Defense, War, and Nuclear Weapons Programs

The simplified breakdown allows students to compare percentages with the programs and understand the relationship of the numbers within the United States and with other countries.

Another good discussion topic is the fact that the U.S. military budget is 46 percent of the total spent by the 30 largest military budgets in the world. (China is the next largest at 8 percent.) Students should use the numbers as a springboard for their own research and reflection.

An essential baseline in the study of military emphasis and its price tag is President Dwight Eisenhower's final address to the country three days before the end of his presidency in 1961. The former military leader made it clear that he was concerned that the U.S. was spending more on military security than the net income of the all U.S. corporations. He warned that the "military industrial complex" could disrupt the balance between private and public economy, cost and hoped for advantage...the clearly necessary and the comfortably desirable... our essential requirements as a nation and the duties imposed by the nation upon the individual...and actions of the moment and the national welfare of the future."

In a speech to the American Society of Newspaper Editors early in his presidency (from which the quote at the beginning of this chapter was taken), Eisenhower also made specific cost comparisons of one bomber equaling a modern brick school in more than 30 cities, two electric power plants serving a town of 60,000 or two fine, fully-equipped hospitals.

It's important for students to note that George Washington, the first general/ president, also worried that an expanded military could be a problem. Encouraging students to compare other political leaders according to military background and military emphasis is another interesting activity.

Although Eugene Jarecki's book, *The American Way of War*, and his movie, *Why We Fight*, promote his argument that the U.S. military is too powerful, the fact that West Point invites him to speak to cadets is interesting. According to an article by Ben McGrath in *The New Yorker*, Jarecki is invited to visit and share his film even though it is critical of the military to show future military leaders that "critical thinking is not insubordination." That is a good anecdote for class discussion about military power and a list of related topics including nationalism, patriotism, conscription, unilateral and multilateral intervention and diplomacy.

A good source for all interested citizens is The National Priorities Project (nationalpriorities.org). Since it was founded in 1982, NPP has provided information about the national budget process. National Priorities Project was nominated for the Nobel Peace Prize in recognition of its work to describe federal spending on the military and promote a U.S. federal budget that represents Americans' priorities, including funding for issues such as inequality, unemployment, education, health and environment.

A worthwhile student project is available through the NPP and American Friends Service Committee film competition called "If I had a Trillion Dollars." Based on the trillion-dollar Iraq war, the young filmmakers explore other uses for that amount of money and create a three-minute film that promotes their ideas. The film project takes President Eisenhower's comparisons of military spending with schools, hospitals, energy and infrastructure of the 1950s to the 21st Century as students explore the dollars and sense of government budgets.

22
WHEN THE MILITARY CAME TO CLASS
BY DIANA HADLEY

"If all you have is a hammer, everything looks like a nail."

—Abraham Maslow, American Psychologist

After I had completed a couple of winter terms, I had the opportunity to expand the nonviolence class from a four-week intensive session to a full semester. With some feeling of accomplishment I tweaked and expanded the syllabus, excited to use the more traditional schedule. I went to class early on the first day to have all my ducks in a row for the new group, but when I entered the classroom I was surprised to see someone already there. He looked older than the students who usually took the class, so I asked him if he was one of my LA 112 students. He wasted no time telling me that he, in fact, was enrolled in LA112; that his adviser had talked him into taking the class to add to the class diversity that his two tours in Iraq would provide; and that he didn't expect to like the class. Pow!

Journalists use the term "burying the lead" to describe communication that gets to the major point so late in the story that a reader might miss it completely. Daniel's point was placed at the end of the message, but it was clear and powerful.

As other students began to arrive, I wondered how many other advisers had sabotaged the class with students who didn't want to take it. Although the first class didn't introduce many controversial issues, I ran every sentence around in my head a couple of times to test it before it came out of my mouth. After class I looked through the syllabus with new eyes—those of someone who has served in the military. It was a huge stretch since I had never imagined being in the military, but it was my best attempt to calculate the effects of nonviolent concepts and strategies on people with diverse backgrounds and experiences.

While I continued to prepare for classes imagining a viewpoint that might challenge the lesson plan but still deserve respect, Daniel was being the good soldier—dutiful to all the assignments and a great resource for class discussion. I was beginning to feel comfortable with the situation when I came to class a couple of weeks later and discovered that Daniel had arrived ahead of me again. I made small talk and laid out the day's materials. I was wondering if he was going to hand me a drop/add form when he asked if I remembered what he had said on the first day about taking the class. I laughed and assured him that a teacher doesn't forget comments like that; and then he said, "I like my math class, too, but this may be my favorite class."

Once again he had buried the lead, but this time it delivered sweet relief. I can't remember how I replied, so I'm relatively certain I didn't say anything profound or clever. I do remember being astounded that material I had selected for class because I thought was it interesting or inspirational also resonated with someone who had served in the military.

As the semester evolved, I know other members of the class and I looked forward to Daniel's unique perspectives on the issues. One day we talked about what we would do if an armed assailant came to the door and started attacking our class. One student said he would hide, and another said he would jump out the window. Students who didn't think those were great ideas for a small room on the second floor were struggling for something better when Daniel said with matter-of-fact calm, "I'd throttle him."

At that time students didn't expect anyone in a class, including a soldier, to be armed, but campus violence was a new reality. The Virginia Tech shootings had occurred the previous year. Our class discussed the probability that Daniel's response would put him at great personal risk . . . but that it might protect the group as a whole. Some students laughed when a couple of their classmates volunteered to provide backup if Daniel went first. Others said Daniel's comments made sense.

Several students observed that without much thought Daniel seemed quick to decide what he would do and comfortable with an action that might put his own life in danger to save others.

There were still many questions. Did his military training contribute to his reaction or would he have chosen that response before he served in Iraq? Was this the best or the only strategy to save the class? How much force was justifiable? How quickly could other people react when they faced danger? Would an organized plan for the possibility of violence help carry out a nonviolent but effective response if trouble actually occurred?

Like many issues there were more troubling questions than definitive answers, and many students realized they had just discovered another gray area. I had the feeling that when they left class that day the discussion would continue in their heads.

The year after Daniel took LA 112, David and I started team teaching, and we continued to invite Daniel to one class session each semester when he was available to add a military voice to a military discussion. In that same vein of seeking truth, we asked Daniel to add his reflections to the part of this story that is his story. His remarks form the next chapter.

23
AN EX-SOLDIER'S REACTION
BY DANIEL GATES

"Warfare produces peace activists. A group of veterans is a likely place to find peace activists."

—*Mark Kurlansky,* Nonviolence: Twenty-Five Lessons from the History of a Dangerous Idea

Coming to Franklin College was a planned move. I had heard tales of soldiers failing to transition from the military to civilian life due to lack of support and overwhelming change, and my transition was made even more difficult since I was returning from my second tour of duty in Iraq.

To mitigate the risk that I'd flounder and run back to the Army, I enrolled in college with a start date immediately following the end of my term of service, and I chose a school that was close to home and in familiar territory. I chose Franklin College. Since my enlistment ended in January, I began my college career in the spring semester of the 2007-08 school year. Due to my mid-year enrollment, I was limited on available classes, and I couldn't take any classes in my major. The school had a schedule of classes waiting for me, and among those chosen by the school for its only veteran student (at the time) was "LA 112 – Nonviolence." I thought, "No way this is coincidence," and I'm sure I rolled my eyes. "Great," I thought to myself. "First the Army, now the college, is trying to brainwash me."

I told everyone—my parents, my roommate, my brothers and sisters, my friends, some random guy at Starbucks—about how upset I was that the school would try to pull something like this on me. I could tell you that I was unaware of the add/drop process, and that's why I didn't change my schedule, but I tried to. The alternatives, which I can remember only vaguely, were even less appealing to me than listening to a professor wax loquacious about how the military is a useless brute relic, and how we should hold hands and hug trees. I was pretty sure I'd hate the class, but thought maybe I could instigate discussion and provide a viewpoint that Franklin College probably hadn't seen since the end of the Gulf War.

I arrived early. As much as I thought I'd dislike the class I could never intentionally disrespect a professor by being unpunctual. In the nearly empty room I spied the small lady busily preparing for her first day of class. I've been accused numerous times of being too honest. Some call it a type of innocence, others call me a jerk, but either way I felt compelled to inform Professor Hadley that, "I'm pretty sure this is going to be my least favorite class." Looking back, it was a very disrespectful thing to say to a professor on the first day of class, and in this case, it was the first day of a pilot full-semester nonviolence course. Professor Hadley began immediately to practice the very principle her class was about, and with determination and patience she wore down my aggressive and ignorant attitude towards the class.

"Warfare produces peace activists. A group of veterans is a likely place to find peace activists," Mark Kurlansky wrote. While I don't think he's entirely correct, I agree with the premise of the statement. My acceptance of the validity of the course material wasn't gradual. Professor Hadley didn't have to focus on me, or adjust her lesson plan to educate me. Almost from the first day I was convinced.

I'm fond of saying no one hates war more than the soldiers fighting it. They may not all be peace activists, and almost every veteran I've met is proud of his or her service, but they rarely talk about their experiences. When you have good news, or you've had an exciting adventure, or a funny story, you tell as many people as possible. By inference, if a veteran is not willing to share, it's likely the story isn't good, or exciting, or funny. War isn't something a soldier enjoys; it's simply what the soldier does.

Knowing early on that the class was about educating, not converting, certainly helped me accept the material. I enjoyed the class, and it easily became the favorite class of my entire college experience. I enjoyed it so much that when asked to share my experience with the following year's class, I immediately accepted. I'm not sure what I was supposed to add to the class, except to tell my story and answer questions about my experiences in Iraq. I'm sure Professor Hadley hoped that I'd express the effects of her class on me, and I guess I did, although I don't remember it.

Apparently, the moment when I first got the attention of the class was when I said, "I think this should be a required class for all students." I stand by that statement. I think in many cases people choose the violent path due to ignorance. They lack a frame of reference to understand that they have options. Until movies like Zero Dark 30, The Hurt Locker, and Inglorious Basterds are replaced with books like Catch-22, Slaughterhouse Five, and A Farewell to Arms, war and violence will be not only tolerated, but celebrated.

I don't assume that all issues can be solved without physical confrontation, and it would be a disservice to the topic if I tried to preach that. I even spent time coming up with one situation per week that would absolutely require some kind of violent action to solve the problem. That isn't the point of the class at all. The class simply raises awareness that to act in a manner that doesn't require guns or fists is possible. I can't say that I'm an activist, but I know which side of the fire hose I'd be on.

24
WHAT DOES POVERTY LOOK LIKE?
BY DIANA HADLEY

"Poverty is the worst form of violence."

—*Mahatma Gandhi,* 20ᵗʰ *Century Peace Activist*

My husband and I live on the opposite side of a large city from our daughter. The specific place isn't important. It could be any large city. There are two routes to my daughter's house that take exactly the same drive time. One route goes through middle- to upper-middle-class neighborhoods that have landscaped lawns and trees with beautiful seasonal blossoms. Throughout the year it's a pleasant trip that lifts my spirits. The other route goes through a depressed area where the crime rate is higher, and residents are more visible as their tired-looking bodies navigate the sidewalks to and from businesses and homes in need of repairs.

THE PEACE CLASS *A study of effective cheek-turning, neighbor-loving and sword-to-plowshare conversion*

It's not hard to guess which route I prefer. I'm not afraid to drive through the poorer area, but frustration builds by the block when I travel that route and wonder why a city that can support mega-million-dollar athletic facilities can't improve the neighborhoods of all its citizens.

I think more would be done to help the poor if more people drove through those neighborhoods regularly and recognized them as part of their own community. However, many people don't ever see them. Gated communities with all the amenities isolate and protect the affluent from feelings of identification or responsibility. Their children go to upscale private or suburban schools where there may be some ethnic diversity, but few of their classmates live in poverty. Many suburban kids are persuaded to avoid the "bad part of town."

It's possible for young people to make it to college without realizing that poverty exists in their own "extended communities." I have even taken teachers to visit schools in poor areas and found them shocked at the conditions. Within a few miles of each other, public schools vary from those with glass elevators and entries decorated with mosaic tile mascots to buildings that greet their students with broken steps and classrooms with no air-conditioning. One of the teachers I took to an inner-city school was so moved after the visit that he helped the teacher he had just met apply for a grant to finance some educational initiatives.

I think more people would follow that teacher's lead if they had the opportunity to meet people who exist at the margins and to learn more about the things that accompany poverty, including children who live in a violent environment with poor health care and insufficient diets.

Not long ago I was encouraging a group of high-school student newspaper editors at a journalism workshop to localize national news stories for their papers. I used the national high school dropout rate as a possible topic. A student from a private prep school said the national high-school dropout rate wasn't a story that could be localized at his school because its graduation rate was 100 percent and almost every student planned to attend college. When I asked if dropouts at other schools in his city might affect him indirectly, he said it would just make it easier for him to land a better job. None of the students in the group had any sense that an undereducated, underemployed part of the population would affect them negatively. The students did not really project entitlement attitudes; they just didn't expect the crime and violence of the city's poor areas to reach them at some point, and they didn't feel responsible for any part of it.

Poverty has many layers, so there is much to learn. Students from suburban or private schools also don't realize that inner-city schools produce disproportionately greater pools of students who join the military to escape their poor environment and to achieve economic and educational opportunities. Some students in suburban or private schools have never heard of ROTC, one of the most popular programs in some inner-city schools.

It isn't too late to help students see more of their world thanks to the many opportunities to serve challenged communities. Most cities have faith-based and other nonprofit/community groups that welcome young people to assist with existing programs on a long- or short-term basis. There is nothing quite like an immersion experience to go from merely observing to actually absorbing an issue.

It's important for citizens of a democracy to understand the challenges of all citizens and the overall effect of a society including a segment that cannot thrive. Providing the opportunity to study, interact, and then discuss the challenges of all levels of society is essential if a country is going to flourish.

The issue of poverty and a society's responsibility for it isn't new, and concern from people through the centuries has generated quotes that are great prompts for discussion or reflection essays. Any of the following quotes have the potential to engage students:

"The community which has neither poverty nor riches will always have the noblest principles."

—Plato, Greek Philosopher (428/427 BC - 348/347 BC)

"Where justice is denied, where poverty is enforced, where ignorance prevails, and where any one class is made to feel that society is an organized conspiracy to oppress, rob, and degrade them, neither persons nor property will be safe."

—Frederick Douglass, Civil Rights Activist

"I believe that, as long as there is plenty, poverty is evil."

—Robert Kennedy, U.S. Senator

OTHER RESOURCES

An exceptional resource in this area is Michelle Alexander's book, *The New Jim Crow: Mass Incarceration in the Age of Colorblindness.* Alexander describes the incarceration of those who are stuck in a caste system of race and poverty and cannot afford a good lawyer. (Columnist Leonard Pitts recommended the book with such passion that he offered to buy a number of copies himself to send to people who could not afford to buy one.) Alexander provides information to make the case that a cycle of poverty, crime, violence, incarceration, and broken families is a powerful force from which most people who are caught within it cannot escape.

25
THE POVERTY-VIOLENCE CONNECTION
BY DAVID WEATHERSPOON

"Wars of nations are fought to change maps.
But wars of poverty are fought to map change."

—Muhammad Ali, *World Heavyweight Champion Boxer, Activist*

A few years ago I co-taught an inner-city missions class. The class was designed to teach students about poverty and specifically homelessness. It met during an intensive four-week January session and examined how individuals contribute to homelessness, how society contributes, and what can be done proactively to solve the problem of homelessness.

Many students entered the class with preconceived notions. Several believed the homeless are lazy, or that most of their problems stem from alcohol and other addictions. One young man, Tanner, held these views before taking the class. Tanner was bright but could also be a bit of an instigator and a pain. During the course, though, he was transformed.

One week during the month, a group of students had to spend the night at one of the various homeless shelters in the metropolitan area. On the first day, most students were initially wide-eyed and a bit nervous, even scared. By the end of the week, many did not want to leave. Tanner's group happened to be at the men's shelter when a man who had recovered from his time of homelessness was back sharing his story with those who were still struggling. Before becoming homeless, this man had held a six-figure job as a contractor. He had a family and a nice house, and was living the so-called American dream.

Then tragedy struck. His wife and daughter were killed in a car accident. He lost all sense of purpose and meaning, began drinking heavily, and found himself on the streets. It was only through the assistance of the men's shelter that he was able to pull himself together. The counseling programs that the shelter offered helped him gain back his sense of self and begin to find new meaning and purpose. He found a job, but he had not forgotten where he had been or how easily he had landed there. He returned annually to the men's shelter to share his story and offer hope and inspiration to those still dealing with the various challenges that life had thrown at them.

Tanner was profoundly moved. His opinion of homelessness and his entire outlook on life changed. He went from being a class clown to being one of the most passionate justice advocates among his peers. He continues to this day to find ways to reach out to people who are in need of a ray of hope. Tanner learned that poverty and homelessness are not someone else's problem; finding ways to solve these issues is the responsibility of all of us.

Recently, I was at a meeting that was focused on poverty and health care that included roundtable discussions. Around the table were very bright individuals from all walks of life. But the one I felt contributed the most was Vicky, a woman who had formerly been homeless. Life had dealt her a difficult hand, but through the assistance of some caring individuals and some worthy programs, she was now a homeowner and employed directing a food pantry in her neighborhood and helping people in need.

Vicky shared that one of the major issues is the type of help that's offered. Too many people were donating junk foods that they themselves didn't want. There were few options for good healthy foods.

I suggested that the lack of grocery stores in low-income neighborhoods was a major systemic problem. A woman from the suburbs said, "Grocery stores are privately owned, and they have to be able to make a profit. They might fail in these neighborhoods." I replied that plenty of privately owned companies make millions in low-income neighborhoods through fast-cash agencies, bail-bond offices, and liquor stores. These are realities found in any poor area, and they promote a violent culture. Real resources are in short supply, which leads to health and safety issues not found in most suburban areas. Crime rates escalate in places where everyone operates out of a sense of lack. It is a violent mindset that society has perpetrated on poor neighborhoods.

I was listening to a recent radio broadcast about issues the local city council would discuss. Items for the next meeting included infrastructure, taxes, and panhandling. At such meetings, concerns about panhandling often become discussions about how to move the homeless community out of the sight of other people. The aim is seldom to bring change that would keep these people from becoming homeless in the first place. If a major sporting event is about to happen, the city simply finds ways either to move the homeless to another location or overcrowd the jails for a short time while the festivities take place. These are not solutions.

Our job as teachers is to help students realize the problem is one for which all of us are responsible in some degree, and solving it needs everyone's input. Most people, whether rich or poor, want to have homes of their own and be able to provide the basic necessities for their families. They want safe neighborhoods with good schools and affordable options for health care. These are not unrealistic expectations, and if met, they open the door to less violence and better integration of communities.

26
OUTSKIRTS OF THE CITY: MIGRANTS AND IMMIGRANTS
BY DIANA HADLEY

"History will judge societies and governments—and their institutions—not by how big they are or how well they serve the rich and the powerful, but by how effectively they respond to the needs of the poor and the helpless."

—Richard Griswold del Castillo and Richard A. Garcia,
quoted in A Triumph of Spirit by Cesar Chavez

Teachers at the high school where I taught were encouraged to design curricula incorporating layers of related resources that challenged students to study a variety of perspectives about a specific topic. Students then explored ideas for solutions to contemporary issues related to the subject.

One of my favorite multi-source study units for gifted-and-talented English classes combined John Steinbeck's novels *Of Mice and Men* and *Grapes of Wrath* with Edward R. Murrow's documentary *Harvest of Shame*. Individual assignments and class discussion gave students the opportunity to compare and contrast Steinbeck's story of migrant workers in the 1930s with the poor migrant working conditions Murrow described in 1960 with the *CBS Reports* documentary.

Success of the novel *Grapes of Wrath* was followed by the movie version that starred Henry Fonda. Harvest of Shame was broadcast during a Thanksgiving weekend with Murrow's hope that it would literally "shame" well-fed Americans into demanding better working conditions for the people who provided bountiful harvests. Consequently, a variety of media platforms reached large audiences with information that was new to many.

Both Steinbeck and Murrow told stories that provided voice for the oppressed. Although my students could find many other people and groups who worked passionately and spoke persuasively for the migrants' plight, including Cesar Chavez and members of the United Farm Workers union, Robert Kennedy, and even one of their local newspaper columnists, they were amazed that decades after the publication of *Grapes of Wrath* poor living and working conditions for migrant workers remained.

As we update the nonviolence course, the study of migrant workers continues to be a good-news/bad-news topic. Sources abound about an area that has political interest and should be a concern for all citizens, but despite this migrant workers continue to have low wages, poor living conditions. and little health care compared to others who live in the United States.

One of the most recent resources for this topic provides a strong link to the nonviolence class: *Fresh Fruit, Broken Bodies: Migrant Farmworkers in the United States* by Seth M. Holmes. Holmes, an anthropologist and physician, has worked side by side with migrant workers and analyzed their lifestyle. His experience provides both eyewitness accounts and statistical evidence of the "structural and symbolic violence" of the migrant system that remains an accepted or ignored part of food production in the United States. Holmes' book (published in June 2013) shines a light on the current state of migrant workers that suggests Edward R. Murrow's closing words of CBS's *Harvest of Shame* in 1960 are still true in the 21st Century.

"The migrants have no lobby. Only an enlightened, aroused and perhaps angered public opinion can do anything about the migrants. The people you have seen have the strength to harvest your fruit and vegetables. They do not have the strength to influence legislation. Maybe we do. Good night, and good luck."

RESOURCES

- *Grapes of Wrath*, John Steinbeck, 1939
- *Harvest of Shame*, CBS Reports, 1960
- *Fresh Fruit, Broken Bodies: Migrant Farmworkers in the United States*, Seth M. Holmes, PhD, MD, 2013
- *The Fight in the Fields: Cesar Chavez and the Farmworkers Movement*, Susan Ferriss and Ricardo Sandoval
- *American Exodus: The Dust Bowl Migration and Okie Culture in California*, James N. Gregory
- *The Worst Hard Time: The Untold Story of Those Who Survived the Great American Dust Bowl*, Timothy Egan
- "Stories from the Great American Dust Bowl": NPR @ www.npr.org Fresh Air, WHYY, Dec. 4, 2006
- Government statistics

27
DOMESTIC VIOLENCE
BY DIANA HADLEY

"Do the best you can until you know better.
Then when you know better, do better."

—*Maya Angelou, Author, Poet*

Much to our relief, our good friend and editor gave us positive feedback as he started working his way through our book. He wondered, however, why we had not included a chapter about domestic violence. It was a good question. We have not yet included domestic violence as a specific study unit in our syllabus, but discussions about violence and conflict resolution in other units often give students the opportunity to connect the dots to their behavior and the beliefs that have evolved from their own experiences, including violence in their homes.

Unfortunately, many students' first experience with violence is not a video game or movie but a troubling, maybe even frightening encounter within the walls of their homes where they are supposed to feel safe. Figures vary, but some experts estimate that 15.5 million children are exposed to domestic violence each year. That number may be higher since many people who are mentally or physically abused by family members are too embarrassed or ashamed to report them.

Although domestic violence has become more widely recognized in recent years, it is still an issue that is often under the radar. Defined as "any abusive, violent, coercive, forceful, or threatening act or word inflicted by one member of a family or household on another," it is the equal-opportunity tragedy of all racial, socioeconomic, ethnic, and religious groups. Poverty or substance abuse may elevate the problem, but news coverage of wealthy celebrities who harm or murder their mates provides regular reminders of the prevalence of domestic violence in all walks of life.

Most of us can relate to this problem. My colleagues who teach at elementary, middle school and high school levels frequently have students tell them about violent things that happen at their students' homes. One elementary teacher from a suburban school had a single class with two children whose fathers were in jail because they had tried to kill the children's mothers. Although teachers are obligated both legally and morally to report suspected trouble, agencies that are supposed to protect children are often understaffed; and the legal system tries to keep families together despite the challenges, so a bad situation may not improve. My own report about an abused student validated my concern but failed to solve the problem. In another example from a school-reported situation, a Child Protective Services representative explained that a middle school student was old enough to protect herself from a parent who threatened the family.

My high school teaching career also included less serious but unsettling examples of family conflict gleaned through extracurricular activities with student newspaper, yearbook, and broadcast production. Students frequently spent many hours after school to meet deadlines. Often they were just dedicated to doing a good job, but some told me it was a safe place to be, away from their homes where parents were arguing.

Teachers have a new appreciation for their students' struggles at school when they realize that what should be an unacceptable home situation is their students' normal. Since most people learn interpersonal relationship skills from their parents, it is no wonder that those who grow up watching negative to violent reactions to frustration with others also react negatively or violently.

Consequently, one of the most encouraging aspects about teaching nonviolence is describing new tools to resolve conflicts and seeing how quickly students are intrigued by them. Who isn't willing to try an approach to conflict that might make life less stressful? What's wrong with a compromise that lets everyone involved save face or perhaps even gain something?

The real metamorphosis occurs when students connect the real people they study (and sometimes meet) in a nonviolence class who practice conflict resolution. Then they have new role models who show them how to make a positive difference in their own lives. I have chosen "metamorphosis" as the word to describe the change, but I really think of it as magic.

28
POVERTY, WEALTH, AND WALL STREET
BY DAVID WEATHERSPOON

"In a country well-governed, poverty is something to be ashamed of. In a country badly governed, wealth is something to be ashamed of."

—Confucius, 6th Century BCE Philosopher, Teacher

"The love of money is the root to all evil."

—I Timothy 6:10

Tune into any news station, and you'll hear or see numbers tracking the stock market's movements for the day—numbers that either raise concern or alleviate fears. Different indexes are consulted to verify the validity of these numbers. For most listeners, it's akin to white noise. For others, it's life or death.

Originally, the report was not intended to be offered daily. It was simply a way of offering a periodic measure of the market. However, in an ultra-individualized society that values personal economics above social welfare for the community, the daily stock market reports have become a routine part of the discourse of news This form of news has been misused and serves to further divide listeners into haves and have-nots.

Trickle-down economics was the market's best friend. Banks and wealthy shareholders saw exponential gains in their stockholdings. Individuals were encouraged to invest in retirement portfolios and diversify their options to get a return that would one day be able to sustain them. As millions of individuals did so, the wealth at the top increased astronomically, but the payoff at the bottom was very limited. Pensions disappeared in favor of retirement contributions. Long-term stability of employees gave way to the immediate interests of companies. Trickle-down economics has not only failed to trickle down to people in need, but the tap has actually gone dry as those who gain exponential benefits fail to share corporate profits with those who work for them. It has widened the poverty gap in society. Wall Street has become the manifestation of personal greed run amuck.

JP Morgan, AIG, Bear Stearns, Fannie Mae, and Freddie Mac have been allowed to do what the average citizen would not be allowed to do: default on their loans without major penalties. Not only were they allowed to default, but they were then bailed out by substantial government funds, and the burden fell to the taxpayers and homeowners whose mortgages were under water. Thus began a series of foreclosures that ruined the credit of many people while the banks of Wall Street kept chugging along with few or no repercussions. The phrase "too big to fail" became the mantra of Wall Street and many within Congress. A real explanation of what failing would mean for the out-of-balance institutions was left wanting in specifics.

 It was truly incredible. The economic framework that had propped up the financial giants would have to be maintained. Yet, the social realities created by economic mismanagement of these institutions—growing homeless rates, declining wages, home foreclosures, and rising unemployment—were the costs. The consciences of those in power across the nation were out of sync with the best interests of the people. Wall Street and its allies were certainly not looking to form a more perfect union as the preamble of the Constitution directs the nation and those in power to do.

Realizing the incongruities between the economic power base and the rest of the country, Occupy Wall Street came into being, to protest the wealth disparity and to call for immediate changes in regulation and oversight of Wall Street. Several media outlets worked to disparage and discredit the members of the Occupy Movement who gathered in Zuccotti Park in Lower Manhattan and in other Occupy sites around the country. Derogatory remarks such as "weirdos" and "hippies" described protestors in an effort to suggest they were on the margins of society. However, many of them were well educated and understood from direct experience the misdeeds of Wall Street; some had even been Wall Street brokers themselves. Instead of accepting thoughtful critique, reflection, and a change of course as the Occupy Movement at its roots was suggesting, the powers that be preferred the alternative offered by President Bush: Go shopping more.

The economic monster that had developed needed to be fed instead of challenged. Instead of encouraging consumers to live within their means, they were urged to take out ridiculous mortgages. Instead of saving some of their funds for basic needs or a rainy day, they were instructed by the Commander in Chief to go shopping. Wall Street had become too important to the fabric of society to be allowed to fail, but instead of reworking it into an institution serving the common good, as suggested by the members of Occupy Wall Street, the continuation of business as usual was the goal of the power base. Undermining the resistance of Occupy Wall Street was the first order of business. Despite efforts that have included use of law enforcement, mayoral offices, and other means of removal and misinformation, the Occupy movement has continued to be a gadfly for Wall Street. The movement has become more organized and thoughtful in its approach, and it offers challenges to Wall Street when that institution threatens the economic integrity of the nation and its social interests.

The challenge that Diana and I have when we meet with our students is to help them examine the status quo, understand the economic giants of Wall Street, and question and challenge unethical economic policies that form the foundation of a system devoid of many checks and balances that would limit its power.

It's also important to help students care about the situation when they don't realize the immediate challenge to their own livelihoods and the livelihoods of their neighbors. Our goal is to help them realize that a major movement led by many of their peers is under way. Will they join them in being voices of critique and challenge?

29
IMPRISONING THE PEOPLE
BY DAVID WEATHERSPOON

"The United States imprisons a larger percentage of its black population than South Africa did at the height of apartheid. In Washington D.C., our nation's capital, it is estimated that three out of four young black men (and nearly all those in the poorest neighborhoods) can expect to serve time in prison."

—*Michelle Alexander,* The New Jim Crow

My mother walked to the window of the clerk at the justice center. The clerk informed her that my sister owed a substantial fee of a few thousand dollars for her stay in jail.

She had been arrested years earlier for drug possession and had spent some time in prison. My mother retorted that the bill for that stay had long since been paid upon my sister's release. The clerk told her that, while there was still a record of the amount charged my sister, there was no record of that bill being paid. My mother replied that the system was corrupt because it sought to enslave anyone caught in its grip by unjust fees and penalties. But the clerk didn't budge. The bill needed to be paid.

My mom continued to speak angrily about the injustice she felt was being perpetrated by the so-called justice center. She then said, "Your expectation is that a poor, uneducated woman who was released from jail would soon throw away any record of payment. However, I paid the bill, and I have the receipt." She then slammed the receipt on the desk in front of the clerk and said, "The real criminals are the ones on the wrong side of the bars trying to cheat the poor of their money and their livelihood." The clerk was left speechless by my mother's evidence of a bill paid in full three years earlier.

The scandal of the prison system has grown steadily. Michelle Alexander attributes the astronomical growth in prisons to the spurious "war on drugs." The prison industry has become big business, a business built on the backs of the poor and most often poor people of color. It is predatory and anything but just. News stories continue to surface that show a real gap between people who have means compared to people who do not. Entertainment, political and athletic celebrities are handled with kid gloves even with multiple offenses while poor and minority offenders with minor offenses receive harsh, sometimes brutal treatment from arrest to sentencing.

In addition, there is a false pretense that jails and prisons are meant to be rehabilitation centers where people who were once unable to live in society due to poor choices and offenses can find treatment and recovery. However, this is not the case for most penal institutions; they have become a means of social control based largely on race, poverty and class.

The real commitment is to incarceration. One example: Gov. John Kasich of Ohio began his term looking for ways to privatize several prisons. The goal of such privatized prison systems is to keep them at a high capacity. The only way to do that is to ensure that there are a high number of prisoners. Shakyra Diaz, the policy director of the ACLU of Ohio, challenged the ethics of incentivizing high-capacity prisons. Diaz noted, "In order to have it at 90 percent, you need to be able to make criminals fill it at 90 percent."

When business depends upon an enslaved cohort, the investors find ways to legalize their profit-making industry. It was true of slavery, and it is now true of the prison system. People imprisoned for any offense are easily discriminated against. It is a kind of violence to the fabric of society when people are imprisoned for minimal offenses simply to keep prison occupancy high for the benefit of stockholders. Privatized prison systems are now publicly traded commodities on the stock exchange.

There is a national blindness about those who have been incarcerated. Their treatment is deemed acceptable because it is out of the public view. The reality, though, is that this treatment is unacceptable, and the policy of purposely filling prisons to capacity is unjust. The United States incarcerates more people than any other country in the world including China and Iran. We must make decisions based on the best interests of all our people and not only on the best financial decision for some.

30
THE DEATH PENALTY: OFFICIAL VIOLENCE
DIANA HADLEY AND DAVID WEATHERSPOON

"The profound moral question is not, "Do they deserve to die?" but, "Do we deserve to kill them?"

—*Sister Helen Prejean,* Dead Man Walking, The Death of Innocents

A student asked, "Wouldn't you want vengeance if someone murdered your spouse?" The question is the kind that often surfaces in the death penalty debate. It's also part of the problem with the debate. My response to the student was: "That's why it's important for me to make a rational decision about whether I am for or against the death penalty long before an irrational circumstance occurs."

Let me be clear. I am opposed to the death penalty, but I think it should be decided by the people when we are thinking rationally, and not left to emotional appeals when everything has become irrational. I agreed with the student that if my spouse were murdered I would certainly want vengeance. However, I need to make my decision about whether the death penalty is good or bad for society long before I am put in the heat of a situation that leaves me responding out of grief and anger.

Statistics about countries that use the death penalty and about its effectiveness also raise questions about whether or not the death penalty is useful. According to various sources, the United States is among the top 10 countries worldwide that use the death penalty, and it is the only Western democracy to do so. Keeping company with the United States are China, Saudi Arabia, Yemen, Iraq, Iran, Sudan, and Afghanistan. Human rights are not synonymous with any of these other listed nations.

The belief that the death penalty is a deterrent is faulty. A majority of police believes that it does not serve to deter criminals. Amnesty International revealed that states with the death penalty actually have higher murder rates than states that have abolished it. There appears to be no substantial evidence that the death penalty is a useful threat. There is also great debate about whether or not the death penalty is cost-effective, given the enormous cost for years of imprisonment, appeals, and procedures involved in the handling of death row inmates.

Also, DNA tests continue to show major problems with the death penalty. The tests have helped exonerate some people on death row, and some who already have been executed. It's impossible to give back the time that anyone has unjustly spent in prison, but it's even more appalling when a sentence based on faulty evidence has already been carried out, with the loss forever of the opportunity to overturn the improper conviction.

The pro-life conversation also becomes part of the equation when debating the death penalty. It seems inconsistent to be pro-life before the birth of a baby and then reverse that viewpoint once the baby is born. However, many consider themselves pro-life while also favoring the death penalty. They argue against playing God on one hand while demanding the right to be the Divine Curator of capital punishment on the other.

Students in class are given the chance to debate whether they favor or oppose the death penalty. They present all sides of the data and then decide for themselves whether they personally find the death penalty a useful deterrent and a moral option for the state to use. Most of the time the class remains split following the debate on whether or not they favor the death penalty.

The class debates are lively. Deeply held convictions rise to the surface, but the debates have usually been quite civil and informative. It really would be nice if Congress could watch the class and discover how to carry out a debate about differences of opinion while maintaining civility as the best interests of all are sought. Some students have chosen to change their positions while others have become more convinced of their original positions. But more importantly, they all have learned how to critically engage one of the more challenging moral dilemmas facing the nation.

In the next part of this essay, Diana discusses some resources for study of the death penalty, with emphasis on the experiences of Sister Helen Prejean.

RESOURCES ON THE DEATH PENALTY
—Diana Hadley

Capital punishment was a frequent topic in high school and college debates in the 1960s. Many of the same arguments for and against the death penalty promoted at that time were used again in a recent discussion by my state's legislature despite a half-century to verify or nullify them. Even though statistics and studies vary, there is more solid information available today than ever before about the old arguments. But as in other areas, students must know how to evaluate the sources and sort out fact and opinion effectively.

Sister Helen Prejean is the author of *Dead Man Walking*, a book about her experience as a Catholic nun and spiritual adviser to several men on death row in Louisiana. Both she and her book are excellent resources. Students can benefit from her experience to come to their personal terms with the death penalty.

Prejean has spoken against capital punishment since the 1980s, but she is an unbiased source because her multi-level experience helps her understand and describe all sides of the trauma that capital punishment causes everyone involved. She has witnessed executions and their effect on the victims' families. Her compassion for these families helps her understand when they lash out at her for her stand against the death penalty. Prejean feels their desire for closure with the execution of the person who killed their loved ones and shares their despair when it does not make them feel better.

The opportunity to hear Sister Prejean speak in person and answer questions in a large group setting is a lesson in respect for all sides. She accepts comments that challenge her stand with patience and respect even though she has heard some of the same questions dozens if not hundreds of times. Her demeanor helps everyone navigate the controversial points positively.

Although a book is often better than the movie produced from it, the 1995 film of *Dead Man Walking* is also a good resource. It was critically acclaimed, earning numerous awards including four Academy Award nominations and an Oscar for Susan Sarandon who played Prejean. Prejean says she was consulted throughout the production, and she appreciated director Tim Robbins' effort to make the movie factual.

There are many resources that provide death penalty information. Some have comprehensive facts, even curricula given without moral judgments, while others have definite agendas to promote. Here are some resources David and I found useful.

RESOURCES

The Center for Wrongful Conviction evolved from a Northwestern University Law School project that exonerated 14 convicted persons including Gary Dotson, who in 1989 became the first person in the world to be cleared by DNA evidence. Since the center's founding in 1998, 36 other people have been exonerated. The website describes its past and present activities and directs people to additional information.

Interesting student efforts on death penalty issues include Texas Students Against the Death Penalty, an energetic group trying to abolish capital punishment in Texas, the state with the most executions of any other state by several hundred.

And finally, there is the "eye for an eye" code, a biblical reference that can initiate deeper study of many cultural and faith-based references used in death penalty discussions. Students are often surprised to hear that "eye for an eye" in the Old Testament was meant to be more just than the forms of retribution often employed. Later in the New Testament, Jesus reinterprets the "eye for an eye" code to help people see that retribution is a poor form of healing for anyone. Such references can help students revisit their own faith traditions and cultures and compare them to others.

There are many other references and quotations that can spur discussion. Here are two:

"It should be clear that the death penalty does just the opposite of promoting decency and respect for life. It dehumanizes people and promotes murder. It can never be applied fairly."

—*John Morrison, Guest Columnist, The Tech, MIT Online Newspaper*

"Forgiving violence does not mean condoning violence. There are only two alternatives to forgiving violence: revenge, or adopting an attitude of never-ending bitterness and anger. For too long we have treated violence with violence, and that's why it never ends."

—*Coretta Scott King, Civil Rights Activist*

31
BIG WORLD, LITTLE TIME
BY DIANA HADLEY

"Let's face it—think of Africa, and the first images that come to mind are of war, poverty, famine, and flies. How many of us really know anything at all about the truly great ancient African civilizations, which in their day were just as splendid and glorious as any on the face of the earth?"

—*Henry Louis Gates, Professor, Author*

The Arab Spring was an exciting time to teach a nonviolence class, but the major daily events added the challenge of studying a large continent made up of many countries with different histories, cultures, and relations to current events.

Our colleague Edward Chikwana, who grew up in Zimbabwe, was an amazing resource; but his explanation of colonialism made us even more aware that we didn't have time to do the continent justice in the few days available during a one-semester nonviolence class that was already pushing the seams of its syllabus.

One of the quick-turn-around assignments we have used a couple of times since the Arab Spring is to challenge students to select an African country and research some of the following facts about it:

- Brief history of the country
- Type of government/leadership
- Natural resources/industry
- Economy
- Educational system
- Cultural/religious aspects
- Current state of stability

Students have a few days to gather the information and five to ten minutes to share their findings with the class. To show the connection of the reports to the continent as a whole, students place a sheet of colored paper on their country on a large map of Africa. The color of paper they select is based on whether their research leads them to feel that the country they selected is currently at peace (yellow), at war (red), or in some state of limbo between the two (orange).

As students complete their short presentations and tape up the colors that represent their countries, the map takes on hues of orange and red, and the students begin to understand the magnitude of the vast challenges that affect a vast continent. (Future lessons may be updated to a projected computerized map that can have the countries shaded on the computer as each student determines the countries' situations. But the different colors of paper are workable for now.)

This exercise is an example of Aristotle's belief that "the whole is greater than the sum of its parts." Each student studies just one country, but in a class of 25 students many countries are described, and everyone in the class benefits from the collective effort.

One of the most important things students learn from this group lesson is simply that there is much to learn. While that realization is daunting, they can apply the background questions from this exercise to other countries and continents as news events break. Our goal is that the simple research strategy they have practiced will provide another tool to analyze world situations long after they complete the class.

32
MANDELA AND TUTU: TWO PORTRAITS OF PEACE
DIANA HADLEY AND DAVID WEATHERSPOON

"I dream of the realization of the unity of Africa; whereby its leaders combine in their efforts to solve the problems of this continent. I dream of our vast deserts, of our forests, of all our great wildernesses."

—*Nelson Mandela, Nobel Peace Prize Recipient, South Africa President*

As I wrote this section, a television news brief reported that 94-year-old Nelson Mandela's medical condition had worsened. A few weeks after that came the news of his death. Anticipating the end of his life, an Associated Press story said Mandela would be remembered as a Nobel Peace Prize laureate and a "symbol of reconciliation" throughout the world.

That's true, but those who study nonviolence benefit from the entire story of a man who became frustrated, turned from nonviolence to violence, and then back to nonviolence in an evolution that included a prison sentence of 27 years.

Mandela wasn't the first nonviolent activist to lose patience and turn to violence, but a re-evaluation while he was in prison led to a commitment to positive strategies that in turn led to a South Africa without apartheid and to Mandela's becoming the first black president of the country.

RESOURCES ON MANDELA AND SOUTH AFRICA

In addition to a 30-minute segment about South Africa included in the PBS documentary, *A Force More Powerful*, an inspiring and entertaining resource is *Invictus*, a 2009 movie starring Morgan Freeman as Nelson Mandela and Matt Damon as Francois Pienaar, the captain of South Africa's rugby union team, the Springboks. The story is based on the John Carlin book, *Playing the Enemy: Nelson Mandela and the Game That Made a Nation*. The film is about events before and during the 1995 Rugby World Cup, which was hosted in South Africa following the dismantling of apartheid. (The title, "Invictus," is Latin for "undefeated" or "unconquered," and is the title of a poem by an English poet, William Ernest Henley.)

There are many good books by and about Nelson Mandela. It is interesting to note that South Africans could not read one of the most popular, *Long Walk To Freedom*, when it was first printed in 1963 because it was an offense to circulate the words of a "banned" person. That "banned person" later became president of the country and a leader for world peace.

DESMOND TUTU

Creativity is the tool of any good teacher. When we teach nonviolence, we are continually asking students to think outside the box. Change does not often happen by maintaining the status quo.

During the years when Nelson Mandela was jailed, the struggle to end apartheid in South Africa was spearheaded by Desmond Tutu. Tutu followed in his father's footsteps initially as he became a teacher. However, he soon realized that the unequal education black children were receiving was only perpetuating the system of apartheid, and he decided that he must find another way to use his gifts and abilities in order to defy the injustice of his country.

Tutu became an Anglican priest, and he began to defy the apartheid-led government on the basis of moral stances and protests. Following a brutal scene in 1976 when police opened fire on students who were protesting apartheid, Tutu began to lead peace marches and called on the world to "divest" in South Africa. Divestment was a creative means to grab global attention and persuade countries to remove any investment from South Africa. The strategy had startling success as South Africa quickly began to lose global favor. Worldwide sanctions had crippling effects on the South African economy. It also precipitated the release of Nelson Mandela in 1990 and the first free elections when Mandela was elected president in 1994. Earlier, in 1984, the nonviolent strategy led to Tutu's receiving the Nobel Peace Prize.

Since his involvement in the anti-apartheid movement in South Africa, Archbishop Tutu has been a global teacher of peace, justice, and reconciliation. He has spoken out against tyranny in Zimbabwe, the war in Iraq, and apartheid in Israel. He has also served as mediator in many different forums throughout the world, as his sage wisdom is welcomed to offer insight on navigating the difficult waters of reconciliation. Through it all, Tutu has become synonymous with justice for all. His strong stances against injustice have been difficult pills for many world leaders to swallow, but Tutu has not hesitated to chastise them for their participation in ongoing global violence. He's even asked President Obama to apologize to the world and to Iraqis for the invasion the United States led against their country.

Although his prophetic voice may be unpopular with many world leaders, the masses of poor and disenfranchised have found Archbishop Tutu to be a shining light of hope and justice. He is a role model for those who wish to participate in nonviolence because he has embodied the self-sacrifice needed to be a peacemaker, actively standing in the face of oppression.

33
MENTORING
GOOD CITIZENSHIP
BY DIANA HADLEY

"Never doubt that a small group of thoughtful, committed citizens can change the world. Indeed, it is the only thing that ever has."

—*Margaret Mead, Anthropologist*

A "byproduct" can be defined as "a phenomenon that follows and is caused by some previous phenomenon." That definition seems appropriate for a nonviolence class, the byproducts of which are inspiring examples of the role of citizenship. Far from a child's first associations with the word "citizenship," as a grade for behavior at school or a patriotic expression of love for and duty to one's country, students of nonviolence have the opportunity to learn about hard work and sacrifices made in the spirit of citizenship. These activities can range from improving conditions in small communities to ones that affect the world at large.

Math teachers say they enjoy "watching the lights come on" in the eyes of students who suddenly understand a difficult mathematical concept. A humanities version of that feedback is the student's obvious wonder as he studies people who do good for the sake of something greater than themselves, often at great personal sacrifice with little or no promise of personal reward.

Suddenly, students whose heroes have been traditional celebrities—athletes, rock stars, and actors—are impressed by a scrawny guy in simple clothes who decides to stop eating until people change a bad situation, or a solitary man who walks from the crowd to stand before a line of tanks as a symbol of individual courage against a regime.

Leadership workshops promote the Afghan proverb that "if you think you are leading but no one is following, then you're just taking a walk." The leaders of successful nonviolent movements aren't just taking a walk. Sometimes millions of people are following them—perhaps in an actual march or demonstration or by engaging in a boycott ranging from products like grapes to such things as transportation or business services.

To study examples of leadership that use information and moral appeals to oppose coercion and force is to discover a quiet but effective power that is unforgettable.

It isn't necessary to review extensively following a study unit about Denmark's quiet resistance to German occupation during World War II. After one lesson, students remember how the Danes countered force with solidarity and creative resistance because it was so unlikely, unified, and impressive.

Some of the techniques for resistance are even entertaining as students realize there is a bit of "Hogan's Heroes" within some real nonviolent strategies. (*Hogan's Heroes* was a popular American sitcom from 1965-1971 in which POWs outwitted their captors on a weekly basis.) Like the POWs, the Danes pretended to be occupied mentally as well as physically, while courageously working together to outwit their captors in a variety of ways and save their country from destruction. (It's interesting to note that many of our students have heard of *Hogan's Heroes*, but at this point in the course are completely unaware of the Danes' resistance.)

REVERSING THE CHRONOLOGY: It's helpful to study some large movements backwards to see the specifics of the Margaret Mead quote that emphasizes the words "small" and "committed." Moving chronologically backwards from the 1963 March on Washington takes us to James Lawson teaching techniques in nonviolent action to a small group of college students in Nashville, Tenn. Backwards from the Danes' resistance to Germany takes one to individuals who have a commitment to country and nonviolence that inspires unified, courageous action. Eventually their efforts exasperate the occupying force, and the military leaves the country without its original intention accomplished and with a great deal of frustration.

This "backwards" study encourages a person to contact a congressman to share a minority viewpoint, despite the pessimistic view that there is almost no chance of making a difference—and the optimistic view that it might. Studying "backwards" also provides motivation to keep trying. Most nonviolent movements take time and patience. Reviewing Martin Luther King Jr.'s "Letter from a Birmingham Jail" provides inspiration for new challenges in the 21st century, because the reader is looking backwards at a different movement decades ago.

The night before King was assassinated he foreshadowed his death with a speech that predicted he might not make the entire trip to the winning of civil rights, but he proclaimed that he had been to the mountaintop and could see the Promised Land. The questions for those who study nonviolence are:

What inspires people like Martin Luther King Jr. to see the mountaintop?

And what strategies and personal qualities sustain them to get there?

RESOURCES

- Documentary: *A Force More Powerful*
- Speech: "I've Been to the Mountaintop," Dr. Martin Luther King Jr., April 3, 1968
- Speech: "Letter from Birmingham Jail," Dr. Martin Luther King Jr., April 16, 1963
- Website: Additional material about "The Tank Man of Tiananmen Square," June 5, 1989, can be seen at http://www.youtube.com/watch?v=eyFm2yncnlI
- 1969 Tinker v Des Moines Supreme Court decision that guaranteed free expression for public school students.
- Daniel Elsburg, Edward Snowden and Bradley Manning stories allow students to raise serious questions about situations that provide both historical and current issues.

34
GLOBAL PEACE ORGANIZATIONS
BY DAVID WEATHERSPOON

"War may sometimes be a necessary evil. But no matter how necessary, it is always an evil, never a good. We will not learn to live together, in peace by killing each other's children."

—*Jimmy Carter, U.S. President,* Nobel Peace Prize Recipient

In a world filled with violence, it often seems as though only a few people are concerned with the need for peace. However, this is not the case. A quick Google search will reveal hundreds of organizations dedicated to peace. Swarthmore College has a website dedicated to listing peace organizations around the globe. It's really incredible the number of people who are actively working to make the world a more peaceful place.

The opportunity to be a peace advocate in one of these global organizations can occur at any moment. Recently, one of our students, Torie, was selected to participate in a summer immersion experience in the Republic of Georgia, a country primarily of Orthodox Christians. One of the leaders of her trip, Dan Buttry, is a long-time peace and justice advocate who has served with the Baptist Peace Fellowship, one of the organizations on Swarthmore College's "peace champions" list.

While Torie was in Georgia, some of the majority population were persecuting Muslims trying to pray on Friday. The local imam was being jailed on Fridays during the prayer time. Dan and some religious minority leaders organized a protest in which Torie participated. The protest was a simple march through the city that culminated in gaining the imam's freedom and the Muslim community's right to pray. Torie had not gone to Georgia anticipating she would be actively participating as a peace advocate, but the moment and the intelligent peace organization leadership presented her with an occasion to be a real advocate.

One of the great misperceptions that must be overcome when teaching nonviolence is the belief that no one will join with the person willing to stand for peace and justice. It's quite inspiring to learn that there are great epicenters of peace and nonviolence where creativity and lively engagement are being expressed. Peace organizations cross many boundaries of religion, culture, and creed, and they offer the possibility of building a better understanding of and respect for the global neighbor. These organizations seek to build bridges of intersection while respecting the differences among individuals and communities. Students soon learn that there are many options for participating in peace movements, and each of these options offers new ways to understand and work with people in their own communities in proactive and positive ways.

But the most important thing for most students is to learn that they are not alone if they choose to participate in this work of peace advocacy, even if what they see presented in the media is a deluge of violence and oppression against such advocates. When students understand that others will be with them, their courage and willingness to be peace advocates increase exponentially. Therefore, our job is one of presenting the smorgasbord of peace options ranging from the Peace Corps to denominational peace groups to secular peace movements. When one begins to research peace organizations, the plethora of them actually becomes a daunting task, but it's much more hopeful and exciting than the violence so often presented in the media.

35
PROJECTS AND CHOCOLATES
BY DIANA HADLEY

"*Critical comments by students should be taken in a friendly spirit. Accumulation of material should not stifle the student's independence. A society's competitive advantage will come not from how well its schools teach the multiplication and periodic tables, but from how well they stimulate imagination and creativity.*"

—*Albert Einstein,* Theoretical Physicist

One reason I was excited when the nonviolence class evolved from a four-week winter term to a full semester was the extra time this would allow students to do projects. The goal was to encourage class members to find an area related to nonviolence that interested each of them specifically and to provide a creative outlet for personal research each could develop into a presentation to share with the class.

I gave them a list of possibilities for ideas, but I encouraged them to think beyond the list to subjects or approaches that intrigued them. I anticipated the fun we were going to have as I encouraged them to be creative, and as they responded enthusiastically to share imaginative projects related to non-violence.

I scheduled the projects for the last few days of the semester so that everyone would have ample time to prepare, and then I suffered with the class in a situation that I will compare to eating too many chocolates. A few chocolates are great. A whole box at one time is too much.

Like a couple of chocolates, the first few presentations provided some great variety, but it was the new age of PowerPoint, a nifty way to organize information for a visual presentation—which was a good idea until halfway through 25 presentations that relied on PowerPoint to the extreme. At about No.18, I was ready to jump out of our second-floor window, and I knew the students were, too. I felt sorry for those who were going last, and suggested they tweak a bit with final touches to keep everyone interested.

I visited my "keep and throw away" theory of teaching strategies and concluded that I could keep the projects for the next semester; but I had to eliminate a schedule that had too many projects presented at once, and also find ways to help students think beyond PowerPoint.

David began team-teaching the class with me the next semester, so there was an additional brain to help find better ways to incorporate individual projects. We decided to encourage some students to do projects earlier in the semester and align them with the syllabus. The placing of the American civil rights movement in the syllabus gave students enough time to gather information and plan a project, so this became the starting point. Since some students would have longer than others to work on projects, we offered to provide extra guidance for those who volunteered to go early, making it as fair as possible. And we encouraged students to either move away from the standard Power-Point or find ways to incorporate it without relying on it as the primary structure of their presentations.

One of the first presentations that semester provided a model for others to follow as a student used his interest in music to explore songs that inspired the civil rights movement. As he played them on a keyboard, he described the background of the songs and the significance of the lyrics. His presentation was not only informative, inspirational, and entertaining, but it also established a model of creativity for the rest of the semester.

The civil rights musical presentation and another student's dramatic presentation early in the semester intimidated a few students who said they had no talent, but we encouraged them to find the form that best suited their interests and those of their classmates. Too many musical or dramatic presentations would just have been more chocolates.

When spacing the projects, we've found that students who anticipate a busy schedule at the end of the semester are quite willing to complete projects on the front side of it. And we haven't noticed a marked difference in quality based on the time of the semester the project is completed.

Some of the project ideas are printed below to provide direction, but it's important to evaluate possible projects each semester. Evolving world events provide a steady flow of subjects that help keep the class relevant and fluid.

PROJECTS RELATED TO WAR

- Panel to discuss a specific country relative to recent violent and nonviolent movements
- History of Nobel Peace Prize
- History of League of Nations and/or United Nations
- Peace Corps/AmeriCorps
- Economics of war and peace
- Historical perspectives of war and peace (Sources for thought: *Lies My Teacher Told Me, A People's History of the United States*)
- School of the Americas (history of civil protest)
- Manhattan Project: Scientific and moral considerations before and after use of the atomic bomb (Book, *Shockwave*, Los Alamos Museum)
- Hiroshima Peace Center (or others)
- Cuban Missile Crisis and/or other "near misses" regarding international issues

'PEACEFUL' PROJECTS (ART, LITERATURE, DRAMA, FILM, MUSIC)

- Impact of music on the American Civil Rights movement or Estonia's nonviolence movement
- Influence of films with violent or nonviolent themes
- Meaning and background of peace symbols

HOW THE MEDIA AFFECT PEACE/WAR

HOW EDUCATION AFFECTS PEACE/WAR

ANALYSIS OF HISTORICAL NONVIOLENT DEMONSTRATIONS
(KENT STATE, VIETNAM, EGYPT)

GUN LAWS (COMPARISON OF U.S. AND OTHER COUNTRIES,
STATISTICS OF GUN CRIMES, ETC. POSSIBLE DEBATE FOR 2 OR 4)

U. S. JUSTICE SYSTEM'S EFFECT ON NONVIOLENCE
(DEATH PENALTY, PRISON SYSTEMS IN U.S. AND THROUGHOUT THE WORLD)

THE EFFECT OF POVERTY ON VIOLENCE/NONVIOLENCE

GOVERNMENT POLICIES AND VIOLENCE/NONVIOLENCE
(TORTURE POLICIES, DETENTION FACILITIES, THE GENEVA CONVENTION,
GUANTANAMO BAY, ABU GHRAIB, PRISONERS OF WAR, ETC.)

PEACE CAREERS

WEAPONS OF MASS DESTRUCTION (AGENT ORANGE)

36
EDUCATIONAL RESOURCES AND METHODS
BY DIANA HADLEY

"I like a teacher who gives you something to take home to think about besides homework."

—Lily Tomlin, Actress, Comedian

"Our progress as a nation can be no swifter than our progress in education. The human mind is our fundamental resource."

—John F. Kennedy, U.S. President

My husband and I have been educators for 43 years. While he has taught middle school science and I have taught a variety of language arts and liberal arts classes at the high school and college level, our careers have at least one thing in common: we have learned as much as we have taught—from both colleagues and students, and we want to share tips we have learned with others.

I appreciated the value of collaboration early in my carrer. The only air-conditioning in the school where I taught was in the office and a small teachers lounge. At the end of those first days of my first year many of us would gather in the lounge after school to drink a Coke and share some cool air and stories from our day. Several of us were first-year teachers, so our new experiences and frustrations amused the veterans as we tried to navigate our way to competence.

As my husband and I started taking classes for our master's degrees and attending workshops in our fields, we met people who shared their expertise and strategies that we share now. I'm going to list a Top 6 of them.

RELEVANCE

One of the things that aggravated some of my colleagues in the early 1970s was the issue of "relevance." Students had started questioning the value of some of their subjects when I was student teaching. It was a time of student unrest, and some of the veteran teachers complained that the students were just disrespectful; but one of my education professors told my class of prospective teachers that if we couldn't defend the relevance of a lesson perhaps the lesson wasn't that great. Four decades later I remember and value that observation. I'm a strong proponent of relevance whether I'm teaching journalism, English or nonviolence. It's never a waste of time to take a minute to explain how the lesson relates to the students' educational paths or their lives in general.

TEACHING ENVIRONMENT

When I was in first grade my classroom was no different than when the school was built in the early 1900s. It had oak seats and desks connected with iron braces that were bolted to the floor in straight rows. A neat alignment was assured, and the furniture had proved to be decades sturdy.

By second grade a major remodeling project had transitioned the school to green chalkboards and less flammable floors, desks and chairs. However, all of my elementary teachers still arranged the desks in rows except one who put them in a square so that we could see each other. Traditionalists thought her arrangement was too casual, and the custodians complained that the room was hard to sweep; but I liked it then as a student, and I have liked it ever since for my own classes.

Rows of seats provide an acceptable arrangement for seating charts and interaction between the teacher and students, but it isn't a configuration that fosters good interaction among students. Most of us are assigned classrooms with a variety of furniture and situations, but when it is possible David and I like to have options to put seats in a large circle where it is easy for each student to see and hear us and every student speak.

RESOURCES

Included in the positives of teaching nonviolence is an increase in resources to enhance the course.

David and I use Mark Kurlansky's *Nonviolence: A History of 25 Dangerous Ideas* and David Cortright's *Gandhi and Beyond: Nonviolence for an Age of Terrorism* as required texts for the course. They provide concise histories for a basic structure of nonviolent movements and some of the people who have contributed so much to a variety of nonviolent actions.

However, it's amazing to note the number of new materials that supplement class discussion and projects. With change happening so quickly it's important that the course remain fluid. Some of our favorites are:

A Force More Powerful—PBS documentary with six nonviolent movements described in 30-minute segments. American civil rights and Denmark segments are extremely informative and compelling.

Fog of War—This 2003 Academy Award documentary by Errol Morris is an interview with Robert McNamara, Secretary of Defense for the Kennedy and Johnson administrations.

Shockwave: Countdown to Hiroshima—Book by Stephen Walker.

Freedom Riders—2012 documentary about civil rights bus ride through the South that resulted in news coverage that affected people.

Paper Clips—Documentary about a small rural school's class project that becomes a world-wide learning experience about the dangers of bigotry and hate.

The American Way of War/Why We Fight—Book/documentary by Eugene Jarecki that takes the warning of former President Dwight Eisenhower regarding the military industrial complex and describes how Eisenhower's fear has evolved.

Amazing Grace—2006 feature film about William Wilberforce's nonviolent persistence to stop the slave trade in England.

Satirical writing from humorists—Mark Twain, Will Rogers, Jon Stewart, Stephen Colbert, John Oliver...(Colbert's "Truthiness" sketch is a great discussion starter.)

There are more and more resources available for nonviolent classes, but some are too time-consuming even with an extended 75-minute class. A short section from a movie or documentary is often enough to share a bit of history or introduce a concept and stay within a good time span for the lesson and educational copyright limits.

Snippets of some resources provide a smorgasbord approach that works well for our overall objectives, and although we have seen several of the choices multiple times we try to be personally engaged in them each time. Students aren't fooled for one minute if an instructor is bored with the resource and is just using it as filler for a weak lesson plan.

Most class sessions benefit from multiple learning activities. Within a 75-minute class, segments of 20-30 minute lessons linked with high interest resources provide variety that maintains student interest. If students are looking at the clock, it's time to evaluate the lesson plan or the approach to it.

SPONTANEITY

The special spontaneous moments become some of our favorite classes. There are student questions or comments that are so far off the subject that they require some deft moves to return to the prepared lesson plan, but sometimes a student question or comment may take the lesson to a better place than the original lesson plan. It is possible to tag the idea as a place to return at a later time, but it is often better to go with the energy of the moment and revamp the original plan.

Some days or events also are hard to ignore. I had a tried and true journalism lesson plan about the elements of news ready for the day when I heard there had been a power outage that had affected multiple states including our own. I left home early to get copies of *The New York Times* and *USA Today* to add to my local paper's reporting to point out the elements of news in this important evolving news story. I copied a couple of articles for my students and had the copies on their desks when they came to class that morning. It was so much fun to combine the basics of the lesson I had with the new resources. Most of the students enjoyed the spontaneous addition and groaned when one of their classmates looked at the date on the news story and said, "Hey, this is from today's paper. Don't you plan ahead?"

ASSESSMENT

I am adamant that the days of a letter grade on a test or written assignment with no other feedback should have ended long ago. Every student deserves an honest, thorough assessment for each assignment. I will admit that as an English and Journalism teacher who had an average of 120 students per semester, grading papers could be overwhelming. It wasn't unusual to grade papers at family gatherings or on vacation breaks. I have known teachers who took personal days just to work through a stack of research papers that had to be turned around quickly at the end of the semester. One of my friends who sneaked papers in her luggage to grade on a trip said her husband was convinced that English teachers thought they were on vacation if they were grading papers in another state.

My saving grace for grading papers has been the rubric. I actually thought I had invented the approach until I realized other people were using similar assessments. Spending time to create a list of expectations for an assignment and distributing the rubric when the assignment is made gives students a clearer understanding of what is expected from the beginning and a feedback system that provides specific rather than general evaluations.

David and I use rubrics that often have four or five main sections to help students easily scan a page that evaluates their strengths and weaknesses. Even if a student doesn't get the grade he wants, he may be able to look at the rubric and conclude that he is only weak in one area. It's encouraging to see positive numbers for content, approach and research, for example, and conclude that with some work on writing style a better grade is quite possible.

PROJECTS

David and I require projects to provide an opportunity for students to explore a specific aspect of nonviolence and share their findings with the rest of the class. When it works it is win-win. To improve the chances of win-win we try to schedule the projects throughout the semester to coincide with similar topics on the syllabus. Students have to submit ideas for approval (to make sure multiple students don't have the same topics), and they are supposed to meet with us periodically to show approach and progress. This periodic oversight is time-consuming, but it has the potential to build a positive one-on-one instructor/student relationship, keep the student on task and discourage academic dishonesty by seeing the student's progress from start to finish.

COURSE/INSTRUCTOR EVALUATION

I never open the school's official student evaluations of my class the day the envelope with them arrives in my mailbox. It takes a couple of days for me to get the courage to look at them. I take the evaluations seriously, and I generally do an extra evaluation of my own on which I list lessons and resources used in the course and ask students to describe the ones that impacted them positively and the ones they think could be eliminated.

I'm not as surprised as I used to be, but I always learn something from the evaluations. One of my all-time favorites said, "You are very, very enthusiastic, but I like you anyway."

I got the message. Even though it was laugh-out-loud funny (and enthusiasm is a good teacher trait) an energetic approach may need to be dialed down a bit for a teenager who is taking a first period class that begins at 7:30 a.m.

37
MICHAEL'S BLACK EYE
BY DAVID WEATHERSPOON

*"But I tell you, do not resist an evil person.
If someone strikes you on the right cheek,
turn to him the other also." —Matthew 5:39*

Critical thinking is paramount to nonviolent
action. It is imperative to look at all sides
of a conflict and search for a meaningful and
peaceful resolution that maintains human
dignity and value for all involved. Education is the best
tool available for equipping people to be critical thinkers who look for life-
giving resolutions to the world's conflicts. This is why I teach nonviolence.

The history of nonviolent action, the techniques used in various nonviolent struggles, and the people renowned and unknown who led nonviolent resistance are all necessary in empowering students in the classroom to become proactive leaders who demand a justice that seeks peace and self-worth for all. The assumption that one party has to completely disempower another in order to win must be challenged. The belief that collateral damage is simply part of the price of conflict does not need to be an accepted reality. The long-held dogma that war can sometimes be just should be relegated to the scrap heap of bad methodology via power politics.

Developing a world of leaders trained to do the difficult work of resolving conflict that allows all involved to actually win is the primary objective of our work. The ability and courage to listen to the complaints of all parties and work toward healthy resolutions while preventing the subjugation of one party are desired outcomes for students participating in the nonviolence course.

I am reminded of Michael, who was taking our class. He had been at a fraternity party the previous weekend. When he entered our class, Michael had a noticeable black eye. After class, he approached Diana and me and said, "I guess you noticed the black eye that I have." I said that it was hard not to notice. Michael added that he had been speaking with someone whose drunk boyfriend quickly became jealous. The guy blindsided Michael, but Michael said, "I quickly remembered this class. I decided to stand there for a moment and then walk away."

Michael maintained his own dignity and forced the boyfriend to re-evaluate himself, because the assailant quickly had to deal with the negative pushback of others including his girlfriend. Michael had not been defeated nor had he chosen to allow the conflict to escalate. His cooler head had prevailed, and he proudly shared the story of his shiner with his two professors describing how he had learned a new and better option for handling conflict. Conflicts will occur, but our hope is that students of nonviolence will implement strategies that will not only prevent an escalation but will also defuse the confrontation.

Finally, I teach nonviolence because I am Christian. The life of Jesus influenced both Gandhi and King as well as millions of other followers. Jesus' message of active love permeates the Gospels. Love your neighbor as yourself is one of the two great commands. It assumes that people will know how to love themselves, and from this understanding, they will then know how to love others, treating them as they themselves would desire to be treated.

The opposite of love is violence. Therefore, as a follower of Christ, I find myself in opposition to all forms of violence. Following Jesus is not conducive to living a life of violence. Justifications, then, for violence are hollow and self-serving for the one who claims to be Christian. I believe that to be true to my own tenets of faith I must uphold the teachings of nonviolence.

War has failed humanity. Millions of people have lost their lives and been displaced from their homes. We need to make nonviolent conflict resolution the practiced paradigm. It will benefit everyone in the short and long run. Our hope is that the students of nonviolence will lead this movement.

38
WHAT WE'VE TRIED TO DO
BY DIANA HADLEY

"When I was a student, I studied philosophy and religion. I talked about being patient. Some people say I was too hopeful, too optimistic, but you have to be optimistic just in keeping with the philosophy of nonviolence."

—John Lewis, *Civil Rights Activist and U.S. Congressman*

Looking back to preparation for the first nonviolence class I taught, I remember the concern I had about finding enough materials to interest students for a four-week course. It's ironic that just seven years later David and I fret that a semester is no longer enough time for everything we would like to cover.

Recent years have included daily news events from the Arab Spring to Osama bin Laden's death to Syria that crowd our lesson plans with important relevant topics. Although we lead the class, we remain students of nonviolence ourselves as we discover new stories and resources about successful resistance to violence. As we add new information, we attempt to save areas of study that students have appreciated in previous semesters. Consequently, every syllabus is different, and we build each one with feedback from our students and the idea that it must remain flexible enough to include new developments.

We would like to increase the number of nonviolent classes and encourage other schools to teach them. Unfortunately, the enthusiasm David and I share doesn't align with a national educational trend to reduce the number of hours for a bachelor of arts degree. It's frustrating to realize that, just as we discover an elective we believe every person should have the opportunity to take, a one-two punch of budget constraints and the current direction of curriculum make the effort to establish more electives at both college and high school levels harder to accomplish.

Our class was no exception. A perfect storm of budget cuts and faculty requirements put our class on the chopping block. Although we tried to keep the opportunity for students by offering the elective as a noncredit workshop experience, the number of students able to attend was less than we hoped. However, the students who attended were engaged with the material and said they appreciated the experience.

A primary reason for writing this book was to make our case for teaching non-violence a priority. We didn't even call it a book in the beginning. For a while it was our "writing project," perhaps more of an in-depth hybrid of editorial and feature story. We wanted to record classroom experiences that we felt compelled to share without setting the bar of "writing a book" so high we would bail out when it became challenging.

From the beginning we realized our "writing project" would not be the first or even the most inclusive book about nonviolence in general or teaching nonviolence specifically. But we hoped that sharing resources, insights, and personal stories about our classes would persuade others to see the need and benefit of classes about nonviolence.

Perhaps this is an untimely leap of faith, in which we're trying to promote nonviolence at the very moment when university and high school elective classes are challenged, when entertainment reaches a pinnacle of violence, when gun ownership is increasing, and when the majority of Americans approve of government-ordered lethal drone strikes without due process.

We can try to change the wind with some degree of optimism because we have embraced the philosophy of those who have done so before us in far more challenging and even dangerous circumstances, often with great success.

Many of the stories and quotes from the resources we've studied have taken up permanent residency in our hearts. One of my favorites is from Quakers & Nazis, a book by Hans A. Schmitt. In his conclusion, about the effort of Quakers during World War II to relieve the suffering war causes all victims (including Nazis), he quoted Stephen G. Cary, a former clerk of the American Friends Service Committee: "Even though we are tiny, and even though there is a vast world to mend, it's important that we keep witnessing to what love can do."

Cary's quote is profound, but it was Schmitt's final line that sealed the message for me and sustains my determination to teach and encourage others to teach classes about nonviolence:

"How much more it could do depends on the rest of mankind."

ABOUT THE AUTHORS
DIANA HADLEY

Diana Hadley has been an educator for 43 years and a Quaker for a lifetime. She didn¹t combine the two until 2007 when she started teaching nonviolence as a four-week winter term course at a small liberal arts college. The class evolved from a winter term course to a full semester and then a team-teaching effort with David Weatherspoon that led to this book. Diana and David hope the stories of their experiences will encourage others to provide nonviolence studies to many levels of education.

DAVID WEATHERSPOON

David Weatherspoon served the past ten years as a college chaplain, and during that time he had several opportunities to teach a variety of classes including joining Diana Hadley in the adventure of team-teaching a nonviolence class together over the course of five years. Passionate about the teachings of Jesus, the chance to educate others about the history and practice of nonviolence alongside a good friend in the classroom was an opportunity that David could not turn down.

A STUDY OF EFFECTIVE
CHEEK-TURNING,
NEIGHBOR-LOVING
AND SWORD-TO-PLOWSHARE
CONVERSION

THE PEACE CLASS

by DIANA HADLEY and DAVID WEATHERSPOON

38440794R00125

Made in the USA
Lexington, KY
08 January 2015